THE MISGUIDED HISTORY OF AMERICAN TAXES

The Origins, Rationales, and Madness That Limit Freedom and Reduce Economic Growth

David Newton

E^3 FREE MARKET PRESS

SANTA BARBARA ✛ CALIFORNIA

ISBN: 978-0-578-17395-5

E3 Free Market Press envisions, develops, publishes, and supports original research manuscripts that promote the timeless tenets of entrepreneurship, innovation, private enterprise, ethics, economic growth, business strategy, new venture development, and free market capitalism.

Contents

Acknowledgements

I want to first acknowledge the generous financial support of the E'
Center for Entrepreneurship, Ethics, and Enterprise – which also
includes its strategic partner, the *Western Center for Journalism*
(WesternJournalism.com) whose motto is "Equipping You With The
Truth". I have known its President, Floyd Brown over 15 years, going
back to when he was the first Director of the Reagan Ranch Center
here in Santa Barbara, so it's always great to work with such a
strong team, fully committed to liberty, lower taxes, less government
and free-market private enterprise.

I also want to thank Fred Barnes for his spot-on Foreword in noting
the track record of tax cuts and economic growth over the last 50
years, along with the reasons politicians always balk at proposals to
reduce and simplify taxes. Fred's straightforward style gets right to
the heart of America's misguided history of taxation.

Thanks also to *Young America's Foundation* President Ron Robinson
as well as Andrew Coffin, Director of the Reagan Ranch Center, who
have supported my books and research articles over the last 13 years
by having me speak at over 25 high school and college-university
student conferences on American free market capitalism, innovation
job creation, and entrepreneurship, Your leadership has inspired me
to strive for excellence in communicating the logic of conservative
principles to America's future generations.

Finally, I want to acknowledge my family for all their love, and God
for His hand of Providence on America – truly the most exceptiona
nation on the earth. May we never take our freedoms for granted

Foreword

When Dave Newton asked me to pen a Foreword to his book
)out our nation's *misguided* history of taxes, my only stipulation
as whether he would allow me the minimum of 50 pages I'd need to
rite down all my thoughts and concerns about this very timely topic.
y commentary focuses on the last 50 years of evidence that tax
ductions always lead to economic growth, followed by three
)servations about why cutting taxes is so difficult for politicians. Dr.
ewton covers all the details in the 25 chapters that follow.

Over the past half-century, there have been six significant tax
ıts, each with very similar results. In every case, the economy
ıproved. More often than not, it boomed. There was President
ennedy's 1964 tax cut (the year after he was assassinated) that
ashed the top rate on individual income from 90 to 70 percent. In
)78, President Carter grudgingly signed a cut in the capital gains
.x rate from 49 to 28 percent. That legislation was championed by
little-known Republican House member from Wisconsin named Bill
:eiger. Three years later, President Reagan's across-the-board 25
:rcent reduction in income tax rates became law (the *Economic
ecovery Tax Act*), and the top rate fell from 70 to 50 percent. The
`chitect of those cuts was another GOP Congressman, former
`ofessional football quarterback Jack Kemp of New York.

Then in 1986, Kemp, Reagan, and two Democrats – Senate Bill Bradley and House member Dick Gephardt – teamed up to pas the landmark *Tax Reform Act* that eliminated loopholes and speci. preferences, broadened the tax base, and cut income tax rates agai This time, the top rate dropped to 28 percent. In 1997, Presider Clinton agreed to a cut in the capital gains rate down to 20 percen And four years later, President George W. Bush trimmed income ta rates – Clinton had ratcheted the top tax rate up to 39.6 percent i 1993. Bush cut it back to 35 percent.

Each of these tax cuts had one distinctive similarity, i addition to the economic success they produced. When propose they all triggered ferocious opposition. And it didn't always com from liberals and Democrats. The Kennedy tax proposal was resiste by Republicans who believed it would be a budget-buster by ne bringing in enough tax revenue. Barry Goldwater voted against i Rather than reduce the capital gains rate, Jimmy Carter would hav preferred to raise it. But the economy was suffering from soarir inflation, surging unemployment, and slow growth. He was forced t a bipartisan coalition in Congress to sign the rate reduction.

Reagan's tax cut survived two intense rounds of oppositio: George H. W. Bush (his direct rival for the 1980 GOP presidenti nomination) famously labeled it "voodoo economics" and a cadre senior Republicans agreed with him. Afterward, as presiden Reagan had to overcome fierce Democratic attacks to his philosoph of lower taxes. They predicted an economic collapse if his tax b:

ever passed (see the inside cover of this book's dust jacket). Reagan later said he knew his tax cut was working when Democrats and the media stopped calling it "Reaganomics".

Tax reform appeared to have more opposition than support literally right up to the day it was passed in the Congress. This was because every business interest with a special tax break or a tax subsidy opposed the bill. Most Democrats and plenty of Republicans balked. For it to pass, it required a very popular and influential president such as Reagan to be fully committed to getting it done.

Clinton was no fan of cutting taxes. He ran for office on a message of "middle-class tax cuts", then scrapped the idea once elected. He never talked about capital gains taxes in his 1992 or 1996 campaigns; however, he acquiesced to a cut when Republicans controlled the House and the Senate. Contrary to the forecast of his economic advisers, tax revenues exploded – far exceeding those when the rate was much higher. Clinton did his successor (the younger Bush) no favor by leaving him with a mild recession caused by the bursting of the dot.com bubble. Bush's tax cut, while not deep, was timely, and helped steer the economy back to the growth track.

Just for a moment, think about what has gone on here. When the economy is in trouble, tax cuts are offered as the solution. And indeed, they turn out to be exactly the right solution. Yet whenever cutting taxes to resurrect growth and job creation is proposed again, opponents pour out of the political woodwork. Business interests, unions, academics, liberals, and every recipient of government funds

– they all scream bloody murder. It's as if the repeated record of success for tax cuts has been stuffed down a memory hole. It's as if the tax code in all its complexity is somehow working to the benefit of all of us – while the Internal Revenue Service (the agency in charge of enforcing it) supposedly has our best interests at heart. In the end, even when taxes are reduced, they soon go up again.

I believe there are at least three reasons for this perverse phenomenon. First, there's the misconception that tax cuts are bad for the nation's fiscal health. They might cause inflation, though in recent times they haven't. Conservatives – not all of them – have a special reason for their fear of tax reductions: they make it difficult to balance the budget. Many conservatives are hard-wired to believe in balanced budgets and are offended by deficits. They want spending to be curbed, but that rarely happens. So they're forced either to raise taxes or accept deficits – a terrible choice. They often settle for some of both. But they've begun to see the error of their ways. Many conservatives now favor tax cuts and dismantling the IRS.

The second reason is the proposition that what government does should (must) be paid for. And when government grows (as it inevitably does), the simplest way to pay for it is by raising taxes. Instead of taxing people more heavily, new ways to get tax revenue must be found, and we wind up with an encyclopedia-sized tax code that few people read or understand, creating the need for tax experts, tax accountants, and the IRS. Former House Speaker Newt Gingrich observed that by going along with this system, "Republicans become tax collectors for the welfare state". So true.

The transformation of liberals into progressives is the third reason, because they firmly believe in government with an elite group of bureaucrats and eggheads to run it. They absolutely know what's best for the people – and what's best for the people and government turns out to be the same thing: *more money.* Anyone who watched even one of the recent Democratic presidential debates learned they want to tax the rich to the heavens. Progressives reject free markets because they crave the power and control that ever-rising taxes and spending give them. This then allows for two things: redistributing the wealth to the middle class and poor, while funding vast new government over-spending programs like universal pre-K schools, free college, high-speed trains, and who knows what else. As Claremont scholar William Voegeli says, no matter how much government does, it's "never enough" for progressives.

It should never be this way and it doesn't have to remain as such. Dave Newton explains there are "common sense solutions". We are closer than we've been in years to embracing those solutions. Reagan and Kemp moved us down the path toward lower taxes and a clear and simple system. It will likely take one or two more leaders of their caliber, who learn the lessons that Newton spells out in this book, and we'll finally be home free.

- *Fred Barnes*
Executive Editor, The Weekly Standard

Looking Back At 2017

U.S. TAXES
TIME CAPSULE

(Excerpt from the *Wall Street Journal* March 9, 2042). This week marks the 25th anniversary of the monumental overhaul of the U.S. tax code back in March 2017 which included the 5-year phase-out that shut down the archaic Internal Revenue Service in 2022. The former agency within the U.S. Treasury had become so burdensome and odious to American taxpayers and the U.S. economy due to its 70,000+ pages of regulations and hundreds of millions of hours wasted annually by individuals and businesses filling out mounds of required paperwork from nearly 100 IRS forms and schedules. After several previous bills attempted to reduce some taxes [e.g.: HR-1105 (114th Congress) the Death Tax Repeal Act of 2015] but were vetoed by then President Barack Hussein Obama, the election of 2016 ushered in an administration firmly committed to radical tax reform, with bipartisan backing in the House and the Senate, and huge popular support from American voters on both sides of the aisle. Now that it's been a quarter century, it does seem hard to believe in looking back that our nation was under such an illogical tax-reporting system for just over 100 years – starting with the passage of the 16th Amendment in 1913. Prior to the turn of the century and well into the mid 20-teens, colleges and universities actually used to offer undergraduate and master's degrees specializing in Taxation – as hundreds of thousands of tax accountants, tax attorneys, and investment tax-planning professionals had full-time jobs devoted to knowing the huge federal IRS tax code, how to complete all the forms, and the legal strategies to minimize – or even eliminate altogether – the tax liabilities of individual and business clients. Those born in the last 30 years cannot even imagine what their parents and grandparents had to contend with in that antiquated IRS system. Older Americans will remember filing their own taxes, or hiring a tax-preparer to to the forms, or maybe using an old software package like TurboTax to get everything in before the deadline – when post offices (remember those?) used to stay open until midnight on April 15th so people could mail their tax returns and get that postmark date to avoid penalties for a late filing. You might remember the old Form-1040, 099, Schedule-A, or the W-4, while also trying to figure out which tax rate schedule to use, or what deductions were allowed. Also bygone these 25 years are both the old estate tax (was referred to as the "death tax") – when the government actually took a portion of the assets left to survivors after one's death; and the capital gains tax due on increased market values on stocks, bonds, real estate, and other investments. Compared to today's simple one-page US-1A self-filing form, that old system makes no sense at all. Data from the 2020s and 2030s have shown clearly and overwhelmingly that U.S. GDP, productivity, savings, and investments all increased steadily after the 2017 tax overhaul. The single (and much lower) flat-tax for individuals and businesses turned out revenue neutral from 2017 to 2019, then brought in much larger revenues, especially as the economy improved. Yes, there was a modest 20-month downturn at most accounting and legal firms specializing in tax advice, but in the end, there remained plenty of personal and business bookkeeping, auditing, and financial opinions to keep CPAs busy, while the growing economy had a surge in new capital investment availability. By early 2021 the benefits of the new tax system and the abolition of the IRS had proven to be substantial, as well as sustainable, so in the end it's been a very good thing the last 25 years. So if you're in a thrift or antique store, pawn shop or garage sale, and find a classic 2015 tax code book, or old signboard from an H+R Block office (remember them?), you've got a piece of Americana that just might be worth something for retro-history buffs who collect relics from the past. But thankfully IRS taxes went the way of the iPhone, LG smart-watches, TiVo, Netflix, Segways, and Android operating systems – replaced by clear, innovative thinking that made American taxes a simple and intuitive 10-minute, once-a-year task that's fair and makes sense for everyone. Why we ever did it that old way is beyond me.

Introduction

Taxes have a very complicated history in our country, but do you know the full story behind how we got our crazy tax system, the Internal Revenue Service (IRS), and why it turned into its current broken condition? This book examines the complicated history and evolution of taxation in the U.S. – from the late 1700s to the present. Hopefully it will surprise you, and help you make up your own mind about what needs to be done. And with each type of tax reviewed, we'll examine the same three things: 1) the **Origin** – *when* did each particular tax start? 2) the **Rationale** – *what* was the thinking behind starting each tax? and 3) the **Madness** – *how* did it ever end up in such an illogical and convoluted current format?

When I've asked people, "Do you know when this tax got started?" or "Why do you think they came up with this tax?", they typically reply that they really have no idea how we arrived at our current tax system – and that it's too crazy and far too complicated. Over the last 50 years, numerous political candidates have vowed to finally fix the American tax system, but in the end, very little has changed, except for slight adjustments to rates or some deductions. So the average citizen literally believes nothing can be done.

The idea that virtually all daily purchases, from gasoline to a decaf latte, running shoes to a pizza, include a sales tax; paychecks are reduced by the payroll tax; owning a condo, house, or business facility requires a property tax; making profit on an asset demands a capital gains tax; and each year ends with dozens of forms to fill out to settle payments of both federal and state income taxes, together demonstrate clearly that taxes now invade every aspect of life, with an uneasy feeling there is no recourse, and it will never change.

A person should not have to be a highly educated, well-trained tax accountant or tax attorney to comprehend the dozens of forms, rates, transfers, statutes, exemptions, carry-forwards, adjustments, write-offs, depreciation allowances, and deferral schedules of our existing tax code. Today's taxes, always at-the-ready to step into the lives of private citizens and syphon off portions of personal and business activities, include the following:

- State Sales Tax
- Federal Excise Tax
- County Property Tax
- Federal Payroll Tax
- Federal Income Tax
- State and/or City Income Tax (where applicable)
- Federal Corporate Tax
- Federal Capital Gains Tax
- Federal Gift Tax and Estate Tax ("Death Tax")
- Alternative Minimum Tax,
- and the new Obamacare "Penalty" Tax.

It's truly mind-boggling – *madness* – that there are so many different kinds of taxes – each with its own unique rules about what gets reported, on which form, and paid by which date. It seem inconceivable that the IRS has over 110,000 employees processing over 170 million individual and business tax filings each year, or more than one billion pages – and they are now also responsible for the collection of three different kinds of fees and penalties (taxes related to the federal subsidies on mandated personal heatl insurance policy premiums for Obamacare.

Something is clearly wrong when our tax system has incentives for citizens to minimize earnings and investment gains to avoid paying taxes. Rush Limbaugh recognized that "no nation has ever taxed itself into prosperity" – because lower taxes always incentivize businesses and individuals to pursue *greater* economic activity, while higher taxes always end up discouraging entrepreneurship and innovation. There is overwhelming evidence that America's most prosperous times of growth and job creation occurred when federal taxes were reduced. The strongest recoveries from recession happened when government cut taxes – putting money back into the hands of households and companies so they could invest more, expand operations, make significant new purchases, hire additional workers, increase savings, allocate funds for research and development, pay down debts, and boost salaries and wages. Yet politicians keep saying "it just can't be done", and special-interest lobbyists appear to be too powerful to allow real reform to happen.

This 2016 general election has many of the candidates again talking about the need for major tax reform. That same talk was part of the 2012 election, and 2008, 2000, 1992 – and back to 1962 when President John F. Kennedy told the New York Economic Club: *"The final and best means of strengthening demand among consumers and business is to reduce the burden on private income imposed by our present tax system; I pledged last summer to an across-the-board, top-to-bottom cut in personal and corporate income taxes to be effective in 1963; not a temporary tax cut; I am talking about the accumulated evidence of the last 5 years that our present tax system, developed during World War II to restrain growth, exerts too heavy a drag on growth in peacetime; that it siphons out of the private economy too large a share of personal and business purchasing power; and reduces financial incentives for personal effort, investment, and risk-taking.*

Those are things every American should be free to do – take some risks, invest, work hard, and build income and wealth. This entrepreneurial spirit made the U.S. truly exceptional and financially prosperous. It drives innovation, research and development, robust job creation, and a strong economy. But over the decades, such calls for tax reform always seem to die out once those elected politicians get to the White House, the Congress, or the state house. Entrenched career lawmakers are more concerned about special interest groups and getting re-elected than doing the right thing for all Americans. Government has two major flaws in its logic about taxes. First, that taxes can efficiently redistribute income and wealth "fairly", and second, taxing free enterprise activities will have no negative impacts on those pursuits. I will show how supposedly good intentions lost their way, and how temporary revenue plans ultimately became permanent – why tax rates crept up, tax forms got more numerous (and complicated), and basic tax instructions grew to over 100 pages just to complete the 2-page IRS Form-1040.

The misguided history of American taxes is not about a clearly thought out system that makes sense and functions well. Instead it's 200+ years of patchwork – "add this, tweak that, raise the rates, adjust these, exclude provisions" – with the result being a piecemeal concoction of definitions and special terms that expanded the code to more than 73,000 pages and over 150 different forms (*Wolters Kluwer Standard Tax Reporter*). The system is truly broken and needs to be replaced. My motivation in researching and writing this book was to provide some common sense clarity so that everyone will understand the origins, rationales, and madness that define American taxes – and how these limit our freedoms and reduce great opportunities for economic growth. Thank you for reading, and I hope you will pass it on to your friends and family. NOTE: Even as this book goes to print President Obama has just proposed a new oil surcharge (tax) – in typical government-bureaucrat "tax-more-spend-more" mindset.

> *- David Newton*
> *Santa Barbara, California*
> *January 2016*

Chapter 1

Taxes And The American Founding

Today's Mess Started With . . .
You Guessed It, Taxes!

"Taxation without representation is tyranny."

- James Otis *1775*
Massachusetts Legislature

Origin. The problem with taxes remains the same – the government always begins with supposedly good intentions, but typically these are not very well thought out with respect to the negative effects that will no doubt happen alongside the anticipated benefits. Taxes are implemented, tax codes keep expanding, and the federal bureaucracy becomes increasingly inefficient in its functions – all in the original name of trying to do good. It is then quite fitting that this misguided history starts with the intrusive government of King George's England imposing taxes unilaterally on the thirteen American colonies without any representation from its citizens. The year is 1765, and the British parliament passes the Stamp Act requiring all legal documents, pamphlets, personal wills, newspapers, commercial contracts, even ordinary playing cards, to be 'stamped' in order to demonstrate royal sovereignty of the crown – for which a tax was paid and sent to England. This was quickly repealed, due to the immediate and widespread protest by the colonists. But within two years, the Townsend Act of 1767 put new taxes onto a wide range of goods that the colonies imported directly from England, including paint, glass, paper, metals, and their popular daily drink of tea.

Seven years later, the British East India Company successfully lobbied Parliament for protection from smugglers who were avoiding the formal import tax, and the Tea Act of 1773 was imposed on individuals to ensure that the tax got paid, even if avoided at the port of entry. Protests culminated in the now famous "Tea Party" revolt – where disgruntled colonists dumped an entire ship's tea cargo into Boston Harbor. One iconic taxation-freedom document originating in the American colonies (perhaps second only to the Declaration of Independence) was Thomas Paine's work, *Common Sense* (published January 10, 1776), specifically addressing four majors concerns:

- *The Origin and Design of Government in General,*
- *The Monarchy and Hereditary Succession,*
- *The Present State of American Affairs, and*
- *The Present Ability of America.*

He stated very clearly that is was absurd for an island to rule a continent, and that America was not a "British Nation", within the specific context of securing "freedom and property to all men". The

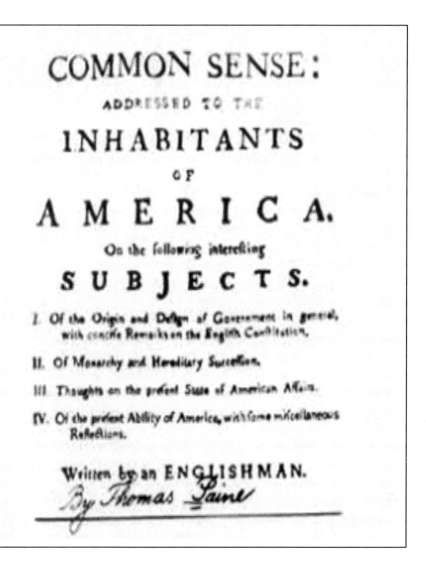

**The Front Cover of *Common Sense*
by Thomas Paine, January 1776**

(Public domain copy at USHistory.org)

pamphlet rapidly galvanized the general population around the idea of independence, with the message going viral throughout the social media of that day – whether by perusing one of the ubiquitous copies circulating from Massachusetts to Virginia, or by hearing its public reading – that the current government was poorly designed, the present state of taxation and other rule without representation was tyranny, and America did in fact have the resources to be successful in its military campaign to oust England from the colonies.

The thirteen colonies did go to war with England, and eventually declared their independence on July 4th 1776. It took an additional seven long years before the 1783 Treaty of Paris formally recognized the United States of America as a sovereign nation. Taxation without representation inspired all kinds of writings, books, songs, and banners to expressly let England know that ordinary citizens would simply not allow a government to unilaterally impose taxes whenever it so chooses. One very iconic symbol among these remains Christopher Gadsden's 1775 flag design showing a coiled rattlesnake with the moniker "Don't Tread On Me" – clearly stating that if England so chooses to proceed in stepping without regard on its own colonies, there would be a swift and violent reaction.

Rationale. Government always presents some supposed form of underlying "logic" behind designing and implementing tax policies. The funds raised are usually designated to remedy some important cause or project that needs to be addressed, so it seems reasonable at first that the country sets aside financial provision for such. But two things tend to be consistently wrong about the rationale for taxes. First, it's assumed that the tax dollars will actually 'fix' the problem – where the cause is taken care of, or the project gets completed. The second misconception is that economic activities of buying, selling, importing, exporting, and earning income will all continue at the same pace and levels in the future, irrespective of the types or amounts of taxes imposed. Both of these rationales wrongly imply only positive effects from such government intervention. The first disregards any likelihood that there could be negative results from federal, state, or local bureaucratic inefficiencies. The second does not truly understand macro- and micro-economics, because taxes and regulatory compliance costs of time and money always reduce private sector productivity, incentives, and investment returns.

Madness. This misguided thinking then assumes that some percentage of new tax drawn from these "normal" transactions will simply take a portion for government without any negative impact on the businesses or individuals involved in the economic activity. But two centuries of research have shown the exact opposite to be the case, as those same businesses and individuals always have to alter their buying, selling, research, and investment decisions in order to accommodate the loss of value siphoned off to pay the taxes. This changes *how much* and *what types* of enterprising risks citizens are willing to accept, because the higher earned incomes must translate to higher and more taxes to pay. Government believes it will influence economic buy-sell decisions by adding tariffs, taxes, fees, penalties, or customs duties to goods and services – as a way to protect certain markets or industries, or to redistribute income and wealth in a supposedly more "fair" manner. Why is it then that politicians are always shocked when higher taxes typically result in lower economic growth and less job creation?

One of the most famous of the founding fathers, Benjamin Franklin, became well known for this very insightful perspective "...but in this world nothing can be said to be certain, except death and taxes". How sad, that such a visionary of these free and united states, would resolve himself – and us – to this bleak reality. So then life in the late 18th century involved the regular reckoning that there can be no doubt, we will all one day die, and in all our days up until that point, we will always be paying taxes to the government. Even more disturbing is that a later chapter in this book examines how taxes actually reach into our personal assets and income *after* the other certainty (death) has already occurred.

That our beloved United States of America owes its very founding to a widespread revolution against an overly burdensome government tax policy is quite an interesting historical fact, because the new nation of freedoms and liberty born from that rebuke of tyranny has now taken 240 years to incrementally add multiple burdens of more and more taxes back onto its citizens. It would be inconceivable to Washington, Adams, Jefferson, Franklin, Paine, and Hamilton that their primary motivation for declaring the states independent of England: overly burdensome taxation, would now dominate every facet of private sector activities and enterprising among households and businesses. Surely the American people are now ready for leadership to not only talk about the negative impacts of excessive government taxation, but to take the necessary *action* to implement true Paine-esque "common sense" remedies that will no longer limit various freedoms and reduce economic growth. The next chapter introduces you to the people – and their income levels – who actually pay all the income taxes in the U.S.

Research and analysis sources include: *TaxFoundation.org; USHistory.org; Encyclopedia.com; Politiact.com; PBS.org; Federal-Tax-Rates.InsideGov.com; TheNewAmerican.com; Bradford Tax Institute; U.S. Library of Congress (LOC.gov); Mark Wilson U.S. Dept. of Commerce Historical Statistics of the United States; IRS.gov; The U.S. Constitution; AmericanThinker.com; Political-Economy.com*

Chapter 2

Meet The American Taxpayers

Well, So Much For Liberty And Justice For All

> *"If Congress can employ money indefinitely*
> *to the general welfare, the powers of Congress*
> *would subvert the very foundation - the very nature -*
> *of the limited government established*
> *by the people of America."*

> *- Alexander Hamilton*
> *First Treasury Secretary*

As a quick break from the timeline about the misguided history of taxes, it's very important to have an understanding of exactly *who* pays income taxes. The range of payers includes all the individuals and businesses that make up the U.S. economy: part-time and full-time workers, small businesses, medium size firms, and large corporations. So then, how many U.S. businesses are there, and how many individuals does the private sector employ? Obviously, the data on our nation's businesses fluctuates annually, quarterly – even weekly. Table 2.1 shows that at any given time, there are approximately 28 million businesses up and running all across our nation, and more than three-quarters of these are sole proprietorships (a single owner with no employees), while less than one-in-four firms have hired employees. Contrary to the "Occupy-Wall-Street" perceptions (dogma) about American capitalism, the majority of individuals in the private sector are *not* employed by giant corporations in the demonized "one percent". In fact, just 3 percent of all U.S. companies employ more than 100 workers.

Table 2.1

PROFILE OF AMERICAN BUSINESSES

Total Businesses	28 million	
Sole Proprietorships	22 million	78% of total
Firms with Employees	6 million	22%
Under 100 Employees	5.8 million	97%
Over 100 Employees	182,000	3%
Over 500 Employees	18,000	
Over 5,000 Employees	2,000	

Sources: U.S. Census Bureau;
U.S. Small Business Administration.

Next, Table 2.2 outlines the U.S. Treasury's collection of personal and corporate taxes over the last seven decades. In the baseline year of 1950, the economy was just under $300 billion and total IRS taxes paid by individuals ($20 billion) and corporations ($10B) were at an

Table 2.2

INCOME TAXES ON THE
U.S. ECONOMY: 1950-2014

	U.S. GDP	PERSONAL TAXES		CORP. TAXES		COMBINED TAXES	% GDP
1950	$293.7B	$ 20B	+	$ 10B	=	$ 30B	10.2%
1960	$526.4B	$ 40B	+	$ 20B	=	$ 60B	11.4%
1970	$ 1.04T	$ 90B	+	$ 30B	=	$120B	11.5%
1980	$ 2.79T	$240B	+	$ 60B	=	$300B	10.7%
1990	$ 5.80T	$470B	+	$ 90B	=	$560B	9.6%
2000	$ 9.88T	$1.0 T	+	$210B	=	$1.21T	12.2%
2010	$14.55T	$1.73T	+	$180B	=	$1.91T	13.1%
2014	**$17.42T**	**$2.35T**	**+**	**$318B**	**=**	**$2.67T**	**15.3%**

Source: Annual U.S. Treasury Report on Spending and
Revenue; U.S. Federal-IRS Income Tax Schedules.

effective rate of 10.2 percent on total GDP – $30 billion taxed on almost $300 billion of GDP. The effective rate is not the actual tax rate charged on personal and corporate income tax returns, but simply the final percentage that the combined tax revenue collected represents compared to the total U.S. economy. Think of that. Up until 1990, the total income taxes collected from all individuals and businesses averaged right around ten percent of the U.S. economy – then increased to over 12 percent in 2000. By 2010 it was around 13 percent, and in 2014 (the most recent data available) it had jumped to more than 15 percent. The continued trend of government's plan is simple – to *spend more* and *tax more*. However, the American tax system is anything but simple in the way that taxes get calculated and paid. Instead, individuals and businesses are required to complete dozens of tax forms, delineating hundreds – yes, thousands – of deductions and additions to their yearly activities, as well as multiple exclusions, exemptions, and adjustments before finally arriving at the actual taxable income, which is then taxed at various rates based upon type of taxpayer and/or level of income.

The next areas for review are the marginal tax rates imposed by government on individual and corporate taxpayers in the IRS tax codes. Table 2.3 summarizes 100 years of the top tax brackets for individual taxpayers. Consider the underlying rationale of that top-end 91 percent marginal tax rate in 1960 – for all taxable income over $400,000. What incentive could there ever be to work hard and generate more personal income if you only keep nine cents on every dollar earned? Yet even for this past 2015 tax year, the top rate remains ridiculously high at 39.6 percent for incomes over $413,000 (single filer), or $439,000 (filing jointly). The only logical, prudent strategy in response to such high rates is to defer as much income until future years (when one might hope that tax rates could be lower) or avoid earning high levels of income altogether. And that's exactly what people did every year to develop and implement personal tax strategies that were specifically designed to legally avoid

Table 2.3

100 YEARS OF PERSONAL INCOME TAX RATES

Top Marginal Bracket

YEAR	RATE
1913	7%
1920	73%
1930	25%
1940	81%
1950	84%
1960	91%
1970	72%
1980	70%
1990	28%
2000	39%
2012	35%
2015	39.6%

Source: U.S. Treasury; The Tax Foundation; Tax Policy Center; Wolters-Kluwer;

paying income taxes when higher rates are counter-productive and serve as a glaring disincentive to pursue profitable economic activities. In either case, these ridiculously high federal tax rates do *not* bring in more revenue from individuals, but rather they serve as a major *disincentive* for being productive and prosperous at work and other economic activity, and eventually result in lower overall tax revenue collected due to formulating lower reported taxable income.

Table 2.4 shows the highest marginal income tax rates for corporations for the last 100 years. In 1950, the IRS imposed a 42 percent "base" tax, *plus an additional 30 percent* on top of that for "excess profits" (1950-1952 prior to the Eisenhower presidency) – as if the federal government could somehow dictate to businesses an exact dollar threshold above which private enterprise was deemed to be earning "too much" (excess) profit. There is no rationale for such an arbitrary cut-off point that discourages growth opportunities. The current U.S. rate of 39.6 percent is the third highest in the world behind Chad and the United Arab Emirates. The average tax rate worldwide is only 22 percent, while Europe averages just 18 percent.

Table 2.4

**100 YEARS OF CORPORATE
INCOME TAX RATES**

Top Marginal Bracket

1913	1%
1920	10%
1930	12%
1940	24%
1950	42% (+30% on "Excess Profits")
1960	52%
1970	48%
1980	46%
1990	34%
2000	35%
2010	39%
2015	39%

Source: U.S. Treasury; The Tax Foundation

Table 2.5 summarizes the proportion of income taxes paid by individuals compared to corporations. In 1950 and again in 1960, the individual/corporate split was 33/67 (one-third from individuals and two-thirds by corporations). Ten years later in 1970, it had completely flipped to 75/25. By 1980 it was an 80/20 split, and remained essentially an 83/17 ratio through 2000. But under the Obama administration it jumped to 90/10 in 2010, and was 88/12 in 2014. Some argue this could be explained by the overall growth in the U.S. population creating more individual taxpayers compared to

Table 2.5

PERSONAL AND CORPORATE TAXES
Share of Total Income Taxes: 1950-2014

	PERSONAL TAXES	% TOTAL	CORP. TAXES	% TOTAL
1950	$ 20B	67%	$ 10B	33%
1960	$ 40B	67%	$ 20B	33%
1970	$ 90B	75%	$ 30B	25%
1980	$240B	80%	$ 60B	20%
1990	$470 B	84%	$ 90B	16%
2000	$1.01T	83%	$210B	17%
2010	$1.73T	90%	$180B	10%
2014	$2.35T	88%	$318B	12%

Source: Annual U.S. Treasury Report on Spending and
Revenue; U.S. Federal-IRS Income Tax Schedules.

the number of taxpaying corporations. However, one thing is clear; a profound fundamental shift has reversed individual taxes from a one-third share compared to corporations, into the current range of 88-to-90 percent. Individuals pay the largest share of income taxes.

Next, it makes sense to see how taxes on individuals are paid across the different income levels. Table 2.61 shows the most recent data for 2013, with the number of taxpayers in each group, and each group's percentage share of the total individual income taxes paid. The top one percent of taxpayers (1,383,000 people) together paid in 38 percent of all income taxes collected (almost 40 cents of each dollar) – while the lower HALF (69 million taxpayers) account for only 3 percent of all the income taxes paid. That disparity is unbelievable.

Table 2.61

**INDIVIDUAL TAXPAYERS
By Income Brackets: 2013**

RANK	ADJUSTED GROSS INCOME	NUMBER OF TAXPAYERS	SHARE OF TAXES PAID
Top 1%	$429,000	1.38 Million	38%
Top 5%	$180,000	6.92 M	59%
Top 10%	$128,000	13.83 M	70%
Top 25%	$ 75,000	34.58 M	86%
Top 50%	$ 37,000	69.16 M	97%
The Rest	*Under $37,000*	*69.16 M*	*3%*

Sources: National Taxpayers Union; The Tax Foundation

Table 2.62 shows similar percentages for 2009. Notice the decrease of 6 million taxpayers (144 million compared to only 138 million in 2013) reflects the continued drop in the labor force participation rate resulting in less income earners working and filing a tax return.

Table 2.62

**INDIVIDUAL TAX-PAYERS
By Income Brackets: 2009**

RANK	ADJUSTED GROSS INCOME	NUMBER OF TAXPAYERS	SHARE TAXES PAID
Top 1%	$344,000	1.44 Million	37%
Top 5%	$155,000	7.21 M	59%
Top 10%	$112,000	14.42 M	71%
Top 25%	$ 66,000	36.05 M	87%
Top 50%	$ 32,000	72.10 M	98%
The Rest	*Under $32,000*	*72.10 M*	*2%*

Table 2.63 goes back another five years to 2004, with 133 million taxpayers (only 5 million less than the most recent data from 2013) - again, demonstrating the lack of significant sustainable job creation due to President Obama's similarly misguided economic policies of massive government spending that have resulted in more than 9 million workers no longer actively involved in the U.S. labor force.

Table 2.63

INDIVIDUAL TAX-PAYERS
By Income Brackets: 2004

RANK	ADJUSTED GROSS INCOME	NUMBER OF TAXPAYERS	SHARE TAXES PAID
Top 1%	$328,000	1.32 Million	37%
Top 5%	$137,000	6.61 M	57%
Top 10%	$ 99,000	13.22 M	68%
Top 25%	$ 60,000	33.05 M	85%
Top 50%	$ 30,000	66.10 M	97%
The Rest	*Under $30,000*	*66.10 M*	*3%*

Finally, Table 2.64 goes back another five years to 1999, with income levels at about the same percentage shares of total income taxes paid.

Table 2.64

INDIVIDUAL TAX-PAYERS
By Income Brackets: 1999

RANK	ADJUSTED GROSS INCOME	NUMBER OF TAXPAYERS	SHARE TAXES PAID
Top 1%	$293,000	1.27 Million	36%
Top 5%	$121,000	6.35 M	56%
Top 10%	$ 88,000	12.71 M	66%
Top 25%	$ 53,000	31.75 M	83%
Top 50%	$ 26,000	63.54 M	96%
The Rest	*Under $26,000*	*63.54 M*	*4%*

For all those news commentators, magazine editors, and web bloggers who regularly bemoan that the upper income earners in the U.S. are "not paying their fair share" of taxes, this data clearly show that to be entirely false. First, about half the tax-filers in America pay no income taxes, due to their relatively low income. That means the top half of wage earners pays virtually ALL the income tax going into the Treasury (96-to-97 percent of the total). Second, less than 1.5 million taxpayers (from a U.S. population of over 300 million) pay in nearly 40 percent of all income taxes. And third, is anyone even concerned that $75,000 of earnings qualifies a person for the top one quarter of all wage earners in this country? I was a full-time college professor up through 2012, and a large share of my recent graduates (2008-2011) working at law firms, hi-tech ventures, Ad agencies, and telecomm companies made north of that $75,000 level – putting them in the top 25 percent of U.S. earners, while still under age 30.

The "occupy" protestors from 2012 perpetuated the false narrative that the top one percent of income earners in America were the mega (filthy) rich millionaires who were hoarding their wealth away and not paying their fair share of taxes. But the previous data clearly show that entrance into the top one percent happened at around $300,000 to $340,000 between 1999 and 2009, and at just under $430,000 in the most recent 2013 results. Granted, there are in fact a good deal of multi-millionaires in that top one percent, but someone making about $35,000 a month ($8,250 a week) is also in that category. And, earning $15,000 a month now puts a person in he top 5 percent of taxpayers, while $10,000 a month qualifies one or the top 10 percent of all American wage earners. This is actually a very sad commentary on the status and recent lack of growth in wages, as the economy has barely increased at an annul 2 percent pace during the last seven years of the Obama administration.

Having found your personal income level in these Tables, then figuring out which earners are above you, and how much more you make than others below you, it's clear that U.S. taxpayers account for very different contributions to the overall tax system. Remember, almost 40 percent of all income taxes are paid come from the top one percent of earners, the U.S. has the third highest corporate tax rate in the world (39.6 percent), and the share of taxes paid by individuals has completely flipped in the last 50-60 years, from one-third, to right around 90 percent today – compared to just 10 percent or businesses. The next chapter introduces you to how taxes were originally collected in the early years of the U.S.

Research and analysis sources include: *TaxFoundation.org; Encyclopedia.com; IRS.gov; Wall Street Journal; PewResearch.org; Political-Economy.com; National Taxpayers Union; Federal-Tax-Rates.InsideGov.com; TheNewAmerican.com; Bradford Tax Institute; U.S. Library of Congress (LOC.gov); Senate.gov/ArtAndHistory; U.S. Dept. of Commerce Historical Statistics of the United States; AmericanThinker.com; CNBC.com*

Chapter 3

Tariffs On Foreign Trade

No, Really, Government Believes It's Helping

*"No taxes can be devised which are not
more or less inconvenient and unpleasant."*   .

- George Washington
President, 1789-1797

The misguided history continued throughout the early years of
the American founding, when tariffs (also known as "customs" and
"duties") were imposed on trade between nations.   Chapter One
showed how the colonies had taxes levied by the British Parliament
to generate income for King George, and to positively influence trade
between the colonies and England, versus other sovereign nations
(like France and Spain).   Tariffs are simply added to the prevailing
market prices of particular goods as a means of discouraging trade
due to this artificially higher cost for buyers.   The nation importing
(buying) the goods is penalized for that transaction when the
purchase price is made higher than goods from another exporter
(seller) without that added on tax. If certain importers still wished to

ay the tariff-increased price, they of course would have to pass that xtra cost along to their customers who buy from them. The tariff ould also be placed on goods being exported as a way to discourage hipments to certain places because the tax makes the price too high nd buyers (importers) will then stay away.

If the goods in question are high-end luxury products that nly the wealthiest can afford, importers might not be dissuaded by he added tariff because their buyers are willing and able to pay that remium price. But if the goods are daily essentials that virtually veryone in the general population buys on a regular basis – specially commodities like cotton, flour, tea, basic metals, wood, obacco, and other agricultural items – then it is highly unlikely that uyers will pay the higher price that includes the tariff, and opt nstead for alternative goods without import customs added on.

One of the main problems with tariffs – like all types of taxes – s the wrong assumption by government that taking what appears to e a small portion of its citizens' regular economic activity as a tax ill not negatively affect that activity. The tax comes off the price, or he income, or the asset value, and there is then no change in the vel of buying or selling – in essence, the tariff has zero impact on ecision making about risk, production, storage, transport, or pricing. ut the reality is that decades of economic research have shown that henever taxes are imposed onto private enterprise, they do adjust he buyers' willingness to pay certain prices, sellers' costs and the vailability of products or services, the wages paid out to workers, and any directly related plans for expansion or new investments. Introducing tariffs into a market changes all levels of trading because the funds lost to the tax have to be factored in to decisions made about supply and demand for products and services.

Tariffs, like all taxes, never happen in a vacuum. In fact, the very structure of customs is intended to alter buying and selling with an artificial increase to the true market price. If you have traveled on an international flight, you'll remember the "duty-free" shops set up between the security screening and the gate area for boarding. That retail square footage is deemed to not be a part of any nation – an entirely neutral locale where no import-export tariffs (the "duty") of any kind are required on the goods bought and sold.

Origin. Tariffs were THE primary form of taxation in colonial times, and continued during the early years of the new nation once England no longer ruled the states. Originally, each colony had its own tariffs as a means to incentivize specific trading, while trying to discourage other trading in certain goods or with targeted partners. When Pennsylvania wished to ensure that rope and twine from its mills would be the preferred product bought by South Carolina, the tariff was added to exports for all colonies except its intended trading partner, so the other colonies would pass on the much higher price, leaving Charleston firms to buy rope and twine at the lower non-tariff price point. In return, South Carolina levied tariffs on its cotton sold to Delaware or New Jersey, but sold to the markets in Philadelphia without that additional cost added to the true market price.

Britain also added tariffs to dozens of everyday goods that the colonies might try to import from France, Spain, or the Dutch East Indies – leaving the English exports for the colonies tariff-free, with a significant price advantage compared to its non-British competitors. These add-on costs ranged from a low of between 10 percent to 20 percent, up to as much as doubling or even tripling the price, making it completely out of the question for the colonies to buy tea or alcohol from anyone other than England. Every ship coming into American ports had tariffs imposed at entry based upon their overall tonnage, essentially charging a flat tax on all goods in the hull.

Rationale. Import-export duties support "protectionism" policies, and are specifically designed to influence certain trade by imposing higher artificial prices on some goods in order to support the markets for those very same goods without the tax. If the aim was to *protect* markets for domestic tobacco or lumber, then any tobacco or lumber coming into colonial ports from outside nations (other than England) would have tariffs added to price these out of the range for fair competition. As the U.S. became a sovereign nation in 1789, the new Constitution banned tariffs and trade restrictions between the states, creating one collective national identity, with tariff-free interstate commerce. However, the use of these customs duties remained the primary taxation for foreign trade.

As a new sovereign country, the U.S. also enacted in 1789 the (Alexander) *Hamilton Tariff* on foreign imports as a way to pay for the basic operations of the new government, as well as to pay down the outstanding debts incurred from the war for independence. The big debates in Congress dealt with which goods were dutiable and which should be left alone. Even back then, the federal government was busy demarcating its long list of customs duties on literally hundreds of products, while others remained tariff-free. Lobbying among states' representatives was intense, to keep some goods flowing freely while others had the case made for this federal tax intervention. The history of the different trade tariffs reads like a series of 'knee-jerk reactions to foreign political moves of the U.S., Britain, and France Every time there was any disagreement on trade, the president and Congress would put into place a new tariff to either punish another nation, or as protection for domestic manufacturers and suppliers.

The new United States of America used tariffs as the main way to raise money for the government, representing on average 80-to-90 percent of all federal revenue from between 1789 up until just before the start of the Civil War. *The Bicentennial Historical Statistics of the United States* (1976) reported the tariff contribution was as high as 97.9 percent in 1825, and still at 94.9 percent in 1860. However, by 1900, tariffs accounted for only 41 percent of Treasury revenues, and in 1915 were just 30 percent. At the onset of the Great Depression (1930) tariffs brought in just 14 percent of all federal funds, and by WWII (1942) had dropped to under 3 percent. Over the last 60 years they have averaged about one percent, as many new taxes have been enacted, and American foreign commercial policy has moved to free rade agreements and the removal of hundreds of tariffs between the J.S. and its import-export partners around the world.

Madness. Even though free trade zones and agreements seem o be the 'norm' in our contemporary world (*NAFTA - North American ree Trade Agreement; WTO – World Trade Organization; CAFTA – Central American Free Trade;* separate deals with South Korea; Australia; Morocco; and the recent *TPP – Trans Pacific Partnership*), he International Trade Commission (ITC) still lists tariffs on over *12,000 products*, covering virtually all dairy and agricultural produce, as well as things like wool clothing, auto parts, leather shoes, neakers, peanuts, tobacco, canned tuna, French chocolates, and apanese leather. Most of these have nothing to do with punishing a oreign nation, but are entirely about protecting domestic American goods and manufacturing. In 2010, the U.S. collected $26 billion in rade tariffs – and while that remains only one percent of all federal ax revenues, an April-2013 *Heritage Foundation* report concluded hat: 1) tariffs make America more poor by transferring dollars from ur most competitive industries, to those with the very best political connections; and 2) low and no tariff countries are consistently more prosperous – with better average incomes – than those with high protectionism' trade tariffs (consider New Zealand and Singapore as he former, vs. countries such as India and Venezuela in the latter).

Perhaps the most interesting historical aspect of British olonial and early American tariffs is that the English Parliament as vell as our *founding fathers* each understood that "taxing" the nation's buying and selling at the wholesale level spread the economic impact more evenly across all of society, no matter the unique income level of individuals. It was presumed that once the tariff was paid on the goods and they were stocked into the wholesale or retail markets, the government's role in taxing commerce was completed, leaving businesses and individuals free to make their own incomes (profits, salaries, wages, commissions) with no additional thoughts of taxation. The discouraging reality is that those 12,000 existing ITC tariffs now have more to do with the politicians and D.C. lobbyists than any positive intentional economic policies. Rather than competing head-to-head, based upon the merit of the goods and services provided, tariffs continue to artificially prop up a wide range of domestic industries and manufacturing – and consumers are the ones who pay the price. The next chapter covers the history of American excise taxes.

Research and analysis sources include: *TaxFoundation.org; Encyclopedia.com; Politiact.com; Federal-Tax-Rates.InsideGov.com; TheNewAmerican.com; Britannica.com; Export.gov; U.S. Library of Congress (LOC.gov); U.S. Dept. of Commerce Bicentennial Edition Historical Statistics of the United States; IRS.gov; The U.S. Constitution; WTO.org/ statistics; OECD-Library.org*

Chapter 4

Excise Taxes

You Want That? It'll Cost You

*"America is a land of taxation, that was
founded to avoid taxation."*

- Laurence J. Peter
Founder, "The Peter Principle"

Having reviewed the taxes imposed on trade (tariffs, or custom
ities), the next topic is excise taxes – sometimes referred to as "sin
xes", based on the line-up of goods typically singled out for such.
ie term "excise" was devised to distinguish this tax from tariffs on
iports, as excise meant the goods were "inland" – already within the
nd (domestically produced).   It is an *indirect tax* (see Chapter Five
imparing direct and indirect taxes) charged to a specific good by a
xed dollar amount, but is not related to the market price of the item.
ir example, today, the excise tax on a pack of 20 cigarettes sold in
alifornia is 87 cents, it's $2.83 in Minnesota, a very high $4.53 in
ew York, but only 17 cents per pack in Missouri. This is different
om an *ad valorem* tax that is not a dollar amount, but a *percentage*

of the selling price, the same as the 8 percent state sales tax here

Santa Barbara County, California – it is always that same consiste

proportion to any taxed good's purchase price.

Origin. The newly ratified Constitution of 1789 stated th

Congress could *"lay and collect taxes, duties, imposts, and excise*

pay the debts, and provide for the common defense and welfare". Th

1789 tariff policy covered in the prior chapter (developed by Treasu

Secretary Alexander Hamilton) also introduced Americans to th

ability of government to *excise a tax* only on 'certain' goods defined

Congress, such as whiskey, snuff, tobacco, rum, and refined whi

cane sugar. But the negative reaction from citizens was immedia

and protests broke out all across the country, culminating in th

1794 Whiskey Insurrection (also known as the Whiskey Rebellio

which resulted in General George Washington leading America

troops to put down the armed civil unrest. By 1802, Preside

Thomas Jefferson noted the revenue collected each year on whisk

was such a relatively small percentage, and outrage kept the ta

extremely unpopular, that he repealed the law with executive orde

much to the delight of hearty bourbon drinkers everywhere.

In those early 1800s, the Napoleonic Wars and then the W

of 1812 contributed to significant reductions in trade with Fran

and then England, resulting in huge drops in tariffs collected. Th

government then looked away from foreign import-export revenu

and focused on implementing excise taxes internally on variou

everyday goods and services. Once these wars passed and trade w

46

normalized, Congress dramatically reduced excise taxes due to trade tariffs again bringing in enough revenue for the federal government to not only cover all its regular operating costs, but also pay down its outstanding debts. In 1834, all U.S. Treasury obligations had been retired, and President Andrew Jackson eliminated all excise taxes, and then cut tariffs in half – because the government had plenty of revenue to pay its bills and the federal debt was now zero. That has

**President Andrew Jackson
(1829 – 1837)**

a wonderful underlying message and tone – government had paid off its debts, and while living within its means, no longer needed certain taxes to remain in place. What a great lesson for today's politicians.

Rationale. The original thinking was fairly logical and did no appear to be too burdensome – that the $4.6 million federal budge could be borne all across the nation's 4 million citizens (as recorde in the 1790 U.S. Census) at on average one dollar and some chang per capita per year on typical purchases. With federal governmen spending limited to the basic operating costs for the president an White House, Congress, the Supreme Court, and the military, th underlying rationale about excise taxes was these small proportion of certain goods were together barely noticeable within market price With the focus on tobacco and alcohol (beer, wine, and liquor) it wa also assumed that a potentially large segment of U.S. citizens woul not even end up paying any excise taxes.

For almost 30 years prior to the Civil War, the U.S. had n excise taxes, only a few limited tariffs, and government operated eac year with a balanced budget. Several years had budget surpluses with the excess funds put into a Treasury reserve (a federal saving account). With the onset of the southern states' seceding from th union and war between the north and south, President Lincoln no only reinstated excise taxes to produce additional revenue for th huge increase in military expenditures, but also introduced in 186 for the first time an income tax proposal (see Chapter Six). The sam rationale persisted and excise taxes remained primarily on alcoho and tobacco throughout the war, then to the end of the 19th centur and continued into the early 1900s. It's also interesting that one c the most prosperous periods of economic growth in the U.S. was in ιe decades after the Civil War, during reconstruction up until 1913, ʼhen there was no regular income tax and the federal government εnerated all its necessary revenues from tariffs and excise taxes.

When prohibition was enacted in 1920 (the 18th Amendment assed in 1919), it marked the end of collecting excise taxes on lcohol for the next 13 years. Then in 1933, Congress passed the 1st Amendment to the Constitution, repealing this prohibition, and ɾesident Franklin Roosevelt signed it into law. It's also worth noting ιat during the Great Depression prior to WWII, the excise taxes on lcohol accounted for an average of 33 percent of all federal revenue.

**President Franklin Roosevelt
(1933 – 1945)**

xcise taxes were greatly expanded by Roosevelt during the 1930s to clude not only the usual beer, wine, and 'distilled spirits' (alongside all types of tobacco products like cigars, cigarettes, chew, and snuff but also commercial trucking, airline tickets, tires, gasoline, an diesel fuel (exhaustive details are in *Historical Statistics of The Unite States*). Essentially the original "sin taxes" and transportation levie accounted for all the excise tax revenue in the 1930s and 1940s.

Gambling has also been a main target of excise taxes. Th British crown allowed the early pre-colonial years of Jamestow Virginia and Plymouth, Massachusetts to use public lotteries to rais funds for deferring the direct costs of these settlements. They we eventually abolished by Parliament, not because of concerns abou the negative effects of gambling, but because Britain knew the lotter reduced the overall cash flow of taxes going back to England. In th early 1800s, New Orleans was the undisputed gambling capital of th U.S. That shifted to San Francisco during the second half of tha century, fueled by the California gold rush. States moved to restri gambling from the end of the Civil War into the early 1900s, but th settling of the western plains and building the transcontinenta railroad gave rise to huge gambling houses in brand new fronti cities like Dodge City, Kansas City, and Denver.

Nevada legalized gambling in 1931 as a measure to reduce th flow of people leaving the state after the majority of its silver min were no longer producing. That, and the Hoover Dam constructic project helped transform Las Vegas (founded in 1905) into a rapid growing city. Maryland made slot machines popular in the years ju after WWII, and New Jersey legalized gambling in Atlantic City i

977. The late 1970s also saw the start of Native American Indian aming on reservation lands, opening the floodgates for states like alifornia to now have casino resorts near Santa Barbara (Chumash), ear San Diego in Temecula (Pachanga), in eastern San Bernardino 3an Manuel), and near Palm Springs (Agua Caliente and Casino lorongo). This continued into online gambling offering poker, bingo, lackjack, sports betting, and new lotteries – reported in 2008 by *H2* *ambling Capital* to account for over $20 billion in revenue worldwide. tates such as Alabama still levy an excise tax on any type of playing ards purchased within its borders – a throwback to when using ards was considered a vice – part and parcel with gambling.

Madness. Today, "sin tax" goods remain targeted for higher xcise taxes every few years (alcohol, cigarettes, gambling, and now larijuana in Colorado). These contribute to illegal unreported sales, s well as smuggling to avoid paying the tax, creating an extension)st of excise taxes to pay for law enforcement needed to track and :ize untaxed goods, and prosecute and incarcerate perpetrators. ozens of newspaper-magazine articles have reported that smokers :main the top target when the federal government wants to raise lore money for "health" related programs. In 2009 the federal excise ix on cigarettes was raised 62 cents per pack - the largest increase l U.S. history. Many published studies over the last 40 years show :rong evidence that excise taxes are disproportionately borne by)w-income taxpayers, which actually makes these one of the most :gressive components of the U.S. tax system.

The IRS conducts thousands of audits every year, trying t ensure that businesses are in compliance with reporting and payin for excise taxable activities. There are over 200 forms that firm must complete to meet excise tax filing and payment deadlines Some of these include: environmental products such as domesti petroleum oil spills and ozone-depleting chemicals; any purchases c trucks, trailers/semi-trailers; all fuels used in business operations multiple types of communications, and air transport. Excise taxe are also due on maritime ship passengers, coal production (a attempt to curtail or even shut down the industry), and cars deeme "gas guzzlers". It requires most companies to have a full-time ta professional either on staff or on retainer who knows all the variou excise requirements, including tax tables, filing deadlines, and forms In conclusion, the dictionary defines the stand-alone word "excise" a *to remove by erasing or crossing out.* How appropriate, as excis taxes do in fact erase (cross out) a portion of one's money. The ne chapter examines *direct* taxes compared to *indirect* taxes.

Research and analysis sources include: *TaxFoundation.org Encyclopedia.com; Politiact.com; Congressional Globe Archives PBS.org; Federal-Tax-Rates.InsideGov.com; TheNewAmerican.com AccurateTax.com; ITEP.org; Investopedia.com; U.S. Library of Congres (LOC.gov); Senate.gov/ArtAndHistory; U.S. Dept. of Commerc Historical Statistics of the United States; IRS.gov; The U.S. Constitution*

Chapter 5

Direct Tax vs. Indirect Tax

You Mean There's A Difference?

*"A national revenue must be obtained,
but the system must be such a one
that while it secures the object of revenue
it shall not be oppressive to our constituents."*

- James Madison
President, 1809-1817

Politicians have certainly been able to dream up all kinds of methods to siphon off taxes from its citizens' economic activities. So far we've examined tariffs on foreign trade and fixed excise taxes added to prices for domestic goods such as alcohol, cigarettes, diesel fuel, gambling, and interstate trucking. This is then an appropriate place to define the difference between *direct* taxes and *indirect* taxes, because the founding fathers were generally united in their thinking that imposing a *direct* tax on individuals would be very invasive to one's personal privacy, and most likely *unconstitutional*, requiring a degree of openness and public disclosure about one's personal finances that would "step way over the line" with regards to

53

protecting individual human rights. Having already clearly define in the Declaration of Independence that people have "certai inalienable rights [and] that among these are life, liberty, and th pursuit of happiness", the original Congress believed very strong] that requiring individuals to give an account of their privat enterprising activities and income for the purpose of taxing thes was most definitely an infringement on personal liberty. The writing of John Adams, Thomas Jefferson, John Hancock, James Madisor Benjamin Franklin, and Alexander Hamilton all have variou arguments and commentaries supporting this thinking.

This *direct* tax is going straight to individual, household, an business entities, and compelling them to give an accounting of thei personal income – or revenues, costs, and operating profit – for th purpose of directly taxing that as it pertains to that one person (enterprise. On the other hand, an *indirect* tax happens during th course of everyday activities that are common to all individuals an businesses – namely buying goods and services. This describes th various state sales taxes, any kind of "per unit" tax, the Europea value added tax (VAT), or the goods and services tax (GST) that popular in many southeast Asian countries like Vietnam, Singapor the Philippines, and Thailand – because while the consumer is th one who bears the ultimate economic burden of the tax, it collected *indirectly* by a commercial intermediary, like a retail store, restaurant, movie theater, public transportation, or a museum.

There are literally dozens of regular daily activities that most mericans do – from filling up the tank at the local gas station, to abbing coffee and a croissant, buying some light bulbs at the ardware store, getting a newspaper or magazine, having lunch with)-workers, picking up dry cleaning and some milk on the way home om work – where every transaction involves the retail-vendor-rovider collecting the taxes on behalf of the government through aily purchases. These are all forms of consumption taxes designed) equally impact each individual consumer or business without gard for their level of earnings or income. The most common of ese indirect taxes today include the following:

- State Sales Tax on all kinds of everyday purchases,
- Federal Excise Tax on gasoline, tires, airline tickets,
- Import Tariffs on foreign clothing, shoes, auto parts,
- GST - Goods and Services Tax on production stages, and
- VAT - Value Added Tax on stages in the production chain.

any presidential candidates over the last 25 years have proposed at the U.S. adopt some form of a GST or VAT to either augment the deral income tax, or to replace it altogether – in essence to raise the ime amount of government tax revenue by taxing the production rocess from raw materials through to the ultimate user, in many ises the consumer. For example, the GST in Australia adds ten ercent to virtually all goods and services purchased. Technically e tax hits every stage of the production process, and is then refunded to each intermediary company up until the final end-user the retail or wholesale party that bears the ultimate payment of th GST. Similar in structure and purpose, the VAT is popular i Europe and from the final buyer's perspective, this tax is levied o the purchase price; however, the seller is only taxed on the "valu added" to a product, material, or service (from an accounting point view) for that stage in the chain of manufacturing and distribution The manufacturer then pays to the government the differenc between those two amounts and keeps the balance in order to offs those taxes previously paid on the various inputs.

It's very interesting to note that another key reason tha America's founders favored the *indirect* tax was that it presse taxation down at an equal rate to even the poorest people in th population; however, proportionately, lower income citizens wou then end up paying the highest de facto *rate* of taxes on their incom compared to middle income earners and the very wealthy. Fo example, if a poor person purchased $8 worth of food each week an paid an indirect tax of 40 cents (5 percent), the poor person with on $10 of total weekly income was then paying that tax at a *rate* of percent relative to his income (40 cents divided by $10). The midd income earner making $18 a week and buying $10 worth of food wit the same 5 percent tax, actually paid just 2.78 percent relative to h income (50 cents divided by $18). The wealthy person making $70 week and buying $25 worth of food ended up paying only 1.8 perce relative taxes ($1.25 divided by $70). The thinking was that th would serve as a motivation for the poorest in society to better themselves and earn more money in order to lower their relative *rate* of taxation. This also was designed to reward those who were industrious and successful in their personal endeavors, by enacting on them a de facto tax *rate* that would decrease as their income rose.

The following excerpt from Thomas Jefferson's private papers captures this very perspective on why the *indirect* tax was greatly favored over *direct* taxes (like a personal or business income tax): "To take from one, because it is thought that his own industry and that

President Thomas Jefferson
(1801 – 1809)

of his fathers has acquired too much, in order to spare to others, who, or whose fathers have not exercised equal industry and skill, is to violate arbitrarily the first principle of association". It is clear that

Jefferson would not advocate the underlying wealth and income redistribution rationale of so many facets in our present tax structure, whereby more types and higher tax rates are chiefly intended to reposition wealth and income away from those who work hard and earn it, over to those whom government deems are entitled to some sort of "fair share" in that targeted wealth and income.

In a very similar manner, Federalist Paper No. 22 shows how Alexander Hamilton most decidedly favored *indirect* taxes rather than a *direct* tax: "It is a signal advantage of taxes on articles of consumption [indirect taxes such as tariffs, sales, and excise taxes] that they contain in their own nature a security against excess. They prescribe their own limit, which cannot be exceeded without defeating the end proposed – that is, an extension of the revenue. When applied to this object, the saying is as just as it is witty that, 'in political arithmetic, two and two do not always make four'. If duties are too high, they lessen the consumption; the [desired] collection is eluded; and the product to the treasury is not so great as when they are confined within proper and moderate bounds. This forms a complete barrier against any material oppression of the citizens by taxes of this class [indirect taxes], and is itself a natural limitation of the power of imposing them. Impositions of this kind usually fall under the denomination of the indirect tax, and must for a long time constitute the chief part of the revenue raised in this country". His point is very well made. If the government taxes directly, it will serve to dissuade individuals (the natural limitation") from earning more, and if the indirect tax is not constrained to a clearly moderate level, it will ultimately reduce consumption of goods and result in lower overall tax revenues.

**Treasury Secretary
Alexander Hamilton
(1789 – 1795)**

In contrast to Jefferson and Hamilton, President Barack Obama is on the record time and again decrying the hard work and economic rewards of entrepreneurship, while advocating higher taxes as a means of redistributing wealth from higher income earners to low-income individuals. Ten years before his 2008 run for the White House, then Illinois state senator Barry Obama said, "The trick is figuring out how do we structure government systems that poo resources and hence facilitate some [wealth] redistribution, because actually believe in redistribution, at least at a certain level to make sure that everybody's got a shot". Ten years later, during his campaign through Ohio he said this during his exchange with Joe (the plumber) Wurzelbacher: "Right now, everybody's so pinched tha business is bad for everybody, and I think when you spread the wealth around, it's good for everybody". In July 2012 while speaking about American private enterprise at a campaign fund-raiser in Austin, TX, he declared, "Look, if you've been successful, you didn' get there on your own; if you've got a business, *you didn't build that -* somebody else made that happen". Such arrogance provides a very clear insight on how he completely misunderstands entrepreneurship and job creation. And the following month (August 2012), speaking at the White House, he added: "...we should ask the wealthies Americans to pay a little more, a modest amount, so that we can reduce our deficit and still make investments in things like education that help our economy grow [because] there are a lot of well-to-do Americans, patriotic Americans, who understand this and are willing to do the right thing ... to do their part to make this country strong".

The public policy of using *direct* taxes (e.g.: income taxes) to raise government funds remains a very divisive topic. The American founders wanted to avoid such an intrusion into the incomes of individuals and businesses, while many contemporary politicians continue to argue for more taxes on households and corporations he largest cut in taxes in U.S. history took place August 13, 1981 when Ronald Reagan signed the Economic Recovery Tax Act (ERTA) 1st north of here at his Rancho del Cielo above Santa Barbara, educing the marginal tax rates on every American by about 25 ercent across-the-board. This is often cited by would be tax eformers as the model-standard for true conservatism in action.

At the time of this writing, the 2016 Republican presidential andidates are all advocating cutting income taxes to foster economic rowth, often invoking President Reagan. Donald Trump (the current ont-runner) proposes eliminating taxes on individuals making less 1an $25,000 and couples making under $50,000 – while closing all ccounting loopholes to ensure that high income investment banks, edge funds, other financial services firms, and wealthy individuals ill pay an "reasonable, appropriate" income tax. Mr. Trump always uips: "My tax plan is going to cost me a fortune", noting that he is ne of those wealthy Americans who uses legal write-offs to reduce is tax bill, but that he and his fellow millionaires should be okay ith paying taxes at a rate around 25 percent, while the corporate 1come tax would drop to 15 percent. The next chapter examines the rst *direct* income tax in America.

---

esearch and analysis sources include: *TaxFoundation.org; olitiact.com; OECD.org; Investopedia.com; U.S. Dept. of Commerce 'istorical Statistics of the United States; WatsonCPAgrouop.com; ?S.gov; Thmas.LOC.gov; FoundingFathers.info; InvestorGuide.com*

Chapter 6

The Income Tax Of 1861

No, Really, This Is Just For The War

*"The democracy will cease to exist
when you take away from those
who are willing to work and give
to those who would not."*

- Thomas Jefferson
President, 1801-1809

Now that we've covered indirect tariffs and excise taxes, an
reviewed how they different from the idea of a direct (income) tax, th
misguided history of modern day income taxes is about to move fror
the philosophical discussions and arguments of Adams, Madisor
Jefferson, and Hamilton – to the first plan to implement such a ta
on the American people. It's remarkable that tariffs and excise taxe
provided funding for all government operations for the first 75 yeaı
of the U.S. as a sovereign nation. Sometimes the excise taxes wer
hiked when foreign trade was not as strong due to geo-politic
issues with England, France, and Holland. At other times the excis

taxes were dramatically reduced (even eliminated) as import duties proved quite reliable in filling U.S. Treasury coffers with plenty of revenue to pay for all government functions in the federal budget.

Origin. By the spring of 1861, President Lincoln and his cabinet were trying to figure out how the northern states Union could afford to engage in war with the southern states who were seceding. It was considered impossible to raise either tariffs, or excise taxes, or both to generate the projected $320 million necessary for a war that was forecasted to last between 12 and 18 months. So the first (direct) income tax was openly proposed. The president dispatched letters to several trusted advisors, including the esteemed Treasury Secretary

**President Abraham Lincoln
(1861 – 1865)**

Salmon Chase, Attorney General Edward Bates, and Secretary of the Navy Gideon Welles – inquiring of them their opinions on whether he had the constitutional right as president to initiate such a *direct* tax. (Let me make a strong recommendation that you read Doris Kearns Goodwin's 2005 national best-seller *Team Of Rivals,* which provides wonderful details about Lincoln's planning and discussions within his bipartisan Cabinet, about this, and other policies and legislation.

Rationale. The early tax debates were very robust and quite animated as the Congress grappled with the issues of freedom and personal property rights, including the constitutionality of levying new and higher taxes on American citizens. The primary argument within the Republican ranks focused on whether the president had the power within the parameters of the Constitution to impose this 'unapportioned' (*direct*) income tax. Remember, when Lincoln was elected in November 1860, all Senate and House delegates from the eleven southern states left Washington, leaving Lincoln's Republican Party with an overwhelming majority in both houses of Congress and the president in the position to move quickly, with very little resistance to both his foreign – and especially his domestic – policies. And while most lawmakers assumed the war with the southern states would be wrapped up in a matter of just a few months, the president was also concerned that as key southern cities and ports came under the jurisdiction of the Confederacy, it would be virtually impossible to try and collect tariffs and other tax revenues.

The arguments for and against the proposed income tax always came back to matters of personal liberty with regard to an individual's income and private wealth. University of Delaware professor Sheldon Pollack notes "To be sure, there was widespread resistance within the Republican Party to all [tax] proposals, most particularly, the income tax, [and] unsurprisingly, conservative Republicans from the northeast [states] adamantly opposed the impost; [and yet] despite this opposition, a majority of Republicans eventually acquiesced to this 'odious tax' based on the need to fund the Union war effort – [in fact] a number of key Republican leaders in Congress preferred this impost over the alternatives, in particular, a national land tax, casting their arguments in favor of the income tax in terms of its 'equity, justice, and fairness' ".

These heavy additional revenue demands of the Union military requirements to thoroughly engage the southern states required that the House and Senate Republicans must accept some type of federal taxation system that (of course) would otherwise be objectionable. There needed to be a compromise to allow for some type of wealth taxation. The options on the table started to favor a direct income tax targeting a broad base of taxpayers, as Justin Smith Morrill of the House Ways and Means Committee motioned it, "the most just and equitable form of taxation", with the forecast being that this tax would raise twice as much federal revenue as any of the previously proposed land tax systems. That would then provide a very strong advantage in light of the severe financial burden facing Lincoln's government in supporting its Union army. One further advantage of a new national income tax was because it would be a "direct" tax, it would not have to be evenly apportioned among the various states based upon population. The heated debates continued to focus away from any kind of proportional land (property) tax, or per capita (population based) tax system, and the *direct* income tax became the preferred method to raise the requisite finances for the war.

The Ways and Means Committee in the House then drew up a bill to tax personal and corporate incomes, and it easily passed in both the House and the Senate, and on August 5th Mr. Lincoln signed *The Revenue Act of 1861* and America had its first federal income tax. However, it was actually not put into operation just yet Income had been defined as "gain derived from any kind of property, or from any professional trade, employment, or vocation carried on in the United States, or elsewhere, or from any source whatever", but the president and his fellow lawmakers were not sure when, or how to implement it, as it created several logistical matters that had not been thoroughly worked out – most notably how it would be collected Congress formally passed the *Internal Revenue Act* on July 1, 1862 with the expressed intention: "to provide internal revenue to support the government and to pay interest on the public debt".

The original terms would have a 3 percent tax on all incomes over $800 – the equivalent of around $23,000 in 2016 earnings However, the actual tax collections, including the income tax, would not happen until September 1, 1862 when the president approved he final version of a progressive 3 percent tax on incomes between $600 and $10,000 – with a higher marginal 5 percent tax rate on arnings over $10,000. The very broad language of the bill was ntended to ensure that essentially *any* earnings by an individual or business would be covered by the law. It's also worth noting that t almost the same time, Jefferson Davis signed into law an income ax for the Confederacy, with the first $1,000 of earnings exempted rom taxes, then a one percent rate up to $2,500 – and finally a two ercent rate on everything above $2,500. The North's income tax as levied on residents of every state and U.S. territory that was not n rebellion. For example, Richmond, Virginia was the site of the Confederate capital, even though northern and western Virginians ere subject to the new federal income tax right from the eginning. States that seceded were again included in the tax base s soon as Union troops regained control of those lands.

Madness. Even though the original intent of this *direct* tax as linked specifically to the expenses of the Union's war with the outhern states, the federal government became quite comfortable ith the new pipeline of revenues flowing into the U.S. Treasury and awmakers tended to assume that if the citizens had become used to aying income taxes, AND with the inclusion of so many added axpayers from the Confederacy, the progressive mechanism and ational collection network of the new law laid the groundwork for he very same payment processes of our modern income tax. In fact, ozens of public newspaper articles, editorials, and other commentaries from the Civil War era all bemoaned how "complicated" it was to figure out one's income taxes, on both the monthly basis and the annual summary basis required in the personal accounting.

Monthly *specific* taxes (fixed) as well as the *ad valorem* tax (a percentage of the market value) were levied on hundreds of products. Monthly taxes were due on the gross sales receipts of transportation businesses, as well as: 1) interest paid on company bonds, 2) the surplus funds accumulated by financial institutions (banks) and insurance companies, 3) gross revenue on public auction sales, and 4) all sales of slaughtered livestock (cattle, hogs, sheep). There were also annual licenses required for stock brokers, bankers, auctioneers, wholesale and retail dealers, pawnbrokers, distillers, brewers, barbers, tobacconists, jugglers, confectioners, horse dealers, livery stables, cattle brokers, tallow-chandlers and soap-makers, lawyers, coal-oil distillers, druggists (apothecaries) photographers and medical doctors. All hotels, inns, and taverns were classified based on the annual (or estimated) rent – from first class to eighth-class establishments. Restaurants (eateries), theaters, circuses, bowling alleys, and billiard rooms paid taxes based on the number of alleys, tables, or seats. Government had already begun to develop its ridiculous bureaucratic abilities to arbitrarily classify virtually every form of business and livelihood . . . for taxation.

The overly detailed enumerations of the final 1862 code laid the initial foundation for the continued madness of today's IRS. All able-bodied individuals, as well as every commercial enterprise, were already recognizing that their income-earning activities were being altered by their logical need to accommodate legal strategies by which to avoid, defer, and reduce their payments of income taxes. The next chapter examines the federal "taxation mindset" that had to develop in Washington, D.C., even as the Civil War continued well past its initial expectations of 'one year to 18 months' and federal spending needed to maintain its budgetary revenue requirements. The income tax stayed in effect in various forms for almost seven years after the end of the Civil War, and was ultimately repealed in 1872, being declared unconstitutional. But you'll ultimately read how it found its way back into the collective life of America.

Research and analysis sources include: *TaxFoundation.org; Sheldon Pollack paper - University of Delaware; Encyclopedia.com; Politiact.com; Congressional Globe Archives; PBS.org; Federal-Tax-Rates.InsideGov.com; Joseph Hill "The Civil War Income Tax"; TheNewAmerican.com; Bradford Tax Institute; U.S. Library of Congress (LOC.gov); Mark Wilson "The Business of the Civil War"; Senate.gov/ArtAndHistory; U.S. Dept. of Commerce Bicentennial Edition Historical Statistics of the United States; IRS.gov; The U.S. Constitution; CivilWar.org; TaxHistory.org; HistoryLink.org*

Chapter 7

The Income Tax Of 1864

After Just 2 Years, Government Wants More

"The power of taxing people and their property is essential to the very existence of government."

- James Madison

The prior chapter examined how the first American income tax (*direct* tax) was designed primarily to generate funds for what federal lawmakers assumed would be about one year (but no longer than 18 months) – to fund the northern states' war with the rebel southern states. However, as the Civil War dragged on much longer than the politicians in Washington had anticipated, it was easy to presume that the once temporary *direct* income tax could then be extended in order to maintain support for the prolonged military campaign. This new "tax mindset" of U.S. lawmakers would become fully entrenched, and – like virtually ALL taxes, fees, and laws – once legislation originally intended to be "temporary" hangs around awhile and gains even the slightest traction within the regular monthly and annual routine of the public sector, it is nearly impossible to reverse the slide into more regulations, let alone abolish the original statute. This same "government knows best" mentality pervades every facet of how federal lawmakers, the states, counties, and cities continue today with this tax-and-spend approach to expanded government.

Origin. With no clear end in sight for the war, and less than 24 months since it was initially launched on September first in 1862, President Lincoln and the Congress on June 30th amended the original law with the significantly updated *Internal Revenue Act of 1864* – designed to expand the government's taxing reach and raise the tax rates, while introducing more specific and larger penalties for enforcing tax payment-compliance. This amended version upped the minimum tax rate to 5 percent for incomes between $600 and $5,000 (cutting the original $10,000 tax ceiling in half), put in a much higher 7.5 percent rate on 'middle' incomes between $5,000 and $10,000 – with the top rate pushed to 10 percent on everything above $10,000. Quite a radical across-the-board tax hike compared to the 1862 law that had a 3 percent rate on income between $800 and $10,000 – and then 5 percent on every dollar over $10,000.

For example, in the prior 1862 law, someone with $4,000 of annual earnings would pay: 1) nothing on the first $800, 2) and then 3 percent ($96) on the $3,200 remaining, for an effective tax rate of 2.4 percent overall on $4,000. But under the new 1864 code, that same person would now pay: 1) nothing on the first $600, 2) then 7.5 percent ($255) on the next $3,400 such that the effective rate jumps to 6.4 percent. These changes were quite radical. Think about it. Persons with the exact same earnings in 1862 and 1864 would see their federal income tax bill go 265 percent in only two years ($255 versus $96). By comparison, that's the same as a person in 2014 having $5,290 in taxes due, and then just two years later, with a new code in 2016, owing taxes of $14,018. A huge increase!

Rationale. There were other substantial changes in the 1864 tax code that helped make it extremely unpopular with Americans. First, the nation was organized into "tax divisions" that sometimes straddled state borders (geographic divisions might include residents of both Pennsylvania and New York) in order to keep clusters of townships and taxpayers in reasonable proximity to the federal tax assessor's 'divisional' office. Second, taxpayers were required to provide a full accounting of their income and assets to the assistant assessor by the first Monday each May – reported on Form-24 that carried the heading: "Detailed Statement of Income, Gains, and Profit (similar to today's IRS Form-1040). If that deadline was missed, the assessor's office would make its own estimate of these values (which was typically much higher than the actual), calculate the income tax due on that best guess, and then add a 25 percent penalty tax for not reporting on time. Consider the prior tax examples. Imagine the $4,000 earner missing the May deadline, having the assessor estimate income at $6,000 ($2,000 higher than actual), then billing the tax at $405 (almost $200 more), then adding on another $101.25 penalty (25 percent) for a total of $501.25 due – double the $255.

A third penalty was that if even one item was found to be in error on the personal income and asset accounting, the assessor would again estimate what were thought to be the correct numbers and re-calculate the updated tax, with a *100 percent* penalty for this kind of 'self-reported' error. In that prior example it would mean another $405 tax on the assessor's estimate. And finally, the tax form stated plainly on the front page *"there can be no appeal"* – so that missing the May deadline, or reporting an error, meant one's taxes would now be determined solely by the divisional assessor, and whatever that amount was, that would be your tax, without any legal recourse. There were no TaxDefensePartners.com, Taxslayer.com, OptimaTaxRelief.com, or IRS Fresh-Start programs to negotiate and settle taxpayer disputes with the government. The assessor's office turned over all tax forms to the Collector of Internal Revenue, who would then post a public notice stating the date and place for final collection of the tax from the payer. The following page shows the 1864 tax assessment for President Lincoln.

Madness. With no appeal rights afforded to taxpayers, they were highly motivated to: 1) make that full accounting as accurate as possible, and 2) get that Form-24 in on time. The penalties (negative incentives) were designed to elicit complete compliance nationwide. Another aspect worth noting is the 1862 law instructed the U.S. Treasury to deduct "anticipated income taxes" from the paychecks of

Figure 7.1

President Lincoln's 1864 Tax Filing

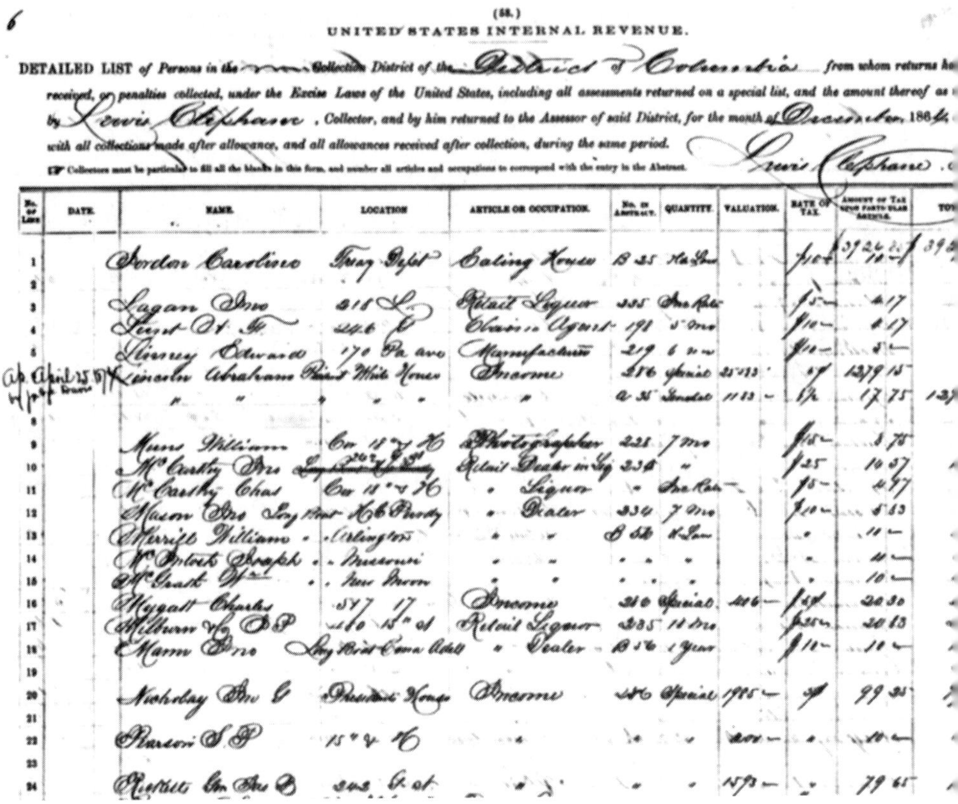

6

(58.)

UNITED STATES INTERNAL REVENUE.

DETAILED LIST of Persons in the Collection District of the District of Columbia from whom returns h[...] received, or penalties collected, under the Excise Laws of the United States, including all assessments returned on a special list, and the amount thereof as [...] by Lewis Clephane, Collector, and by him returned to the Assessor of said District, for the month of December, 1864, [...] with all collections made after allowance, and all allowances received after collection, during the same period.

Collectors must be particular to fill all the blanks in this form, and number all articles and occupations to correspond with the entry in the Abstract.

Lewis Clephane

No. of Line	DATE.	NAME.	LOCATION	ARTICLE OR OCCUPATION.	No. in Abstract.	QUANTITY.	VALUATION.	RATE OF TAX.	AMOUNT OF TAX UPON PARTICULAR ARTICLE.	TO[...]
1		Jordan Caroline	Navy Depot	Eating House	B 35	Half year		$10	39 26 / 10 —	39[...]
2										
3		Logan Jno	218 L	Retail Liquor	335	[illegible]		$5 —	4 17	
4		[illegible]	246 F	Claim Agent	191	5 mo		$10 —	4 17	
5		Linney Edward	170 Pa ave	Manufacturer	219	6 mo		$10 —	5 —	
6		Lincoln Abraham	Presdt White House	Income	256	Special	25583	5%	1279 15	
7		" "	" " "	"	A 35	Special	1183 —	1½	17 75	12[...]
8										
9		Moore William	Cor 11 & H	Photographer	221	7 mo		$15 —	8 75	
10		McCarthy Jno	[illegible]	Retail Dealer in Liq	234	"		$25	10 57	
11		McCarthy Chas	Cor 11 & H	" Liquor	"	[illegible]		$5 —	4 17	
12		Mason Jno	[illegible]	" Dealer	334	7 mo		$10 —	5 83	
13		Merritt William	" Arlington	" "	B 56	Half year		"	10 —	
14		McIntosh Joseph	" Missouri	" "	" " "			"	10 —	
15		McGrath Wm	" New Haven	" "	" " "			"	10 —	
16		Mygatt Charles	577 17	Income	256	Special	406 —	5%	20 30	
17		Milburn & Co D P	410 15th st	Retail Liquor	335	11 mo		$25	20 13	
18		Mann Jno	[illegible]	" Dealer	B 56	1 year		$10 —	10 —	
19										
20		Nicolay Jno G	President's House	Income	256	Special	1985 —	5%	99 25	
21										
22		Parsons S P	15th & H	"	"	"	200 —	"	10 —	
23										
24		[illegible]	303 G st	"	"	"	1593 —	"	79 65	

federal government workers, *including Mr. Lincoln.* But lawmaker re-wrote the follow-up 1864 statute so that federal employees wer then exempt from income taxes (imagine that?) – the thinking bein that government funds were already taxes from the private sector, s it would be double-taxation to pay federal employees with tax dollars, and then require them to pay taxes on those. In fact, Abraham Lincoln's estate filed for, and received, taxes withheld from his pay prior to 1864, reverting his "exempt" status back to the 1862 law.

That thinking was initiated in 1861, then in both the 1862 and 1864 laws it was implemented, that elected officials in Congress, the judiciary, and the White House get self-legislated preferential tax treatments. Clearly that kind of "insiders" federal bureaucratic mindset about taxation has continued, and fostered the misguided history from its inception up to our contemporary broken system. The next chapter explains how this first income tax was repealed only ten years after it was first implemented.

Research and analysis sources include: *TaxFoundation.org; Sheldon Pollack paper - University of Delaware; Encyclopedia.com; Politiact.com; Congressional Globe Archives; Archives.gov; PBS.org; Federal-Tax-Rates.InsideGov.com; Joseph Hill "The Civil War Income Tax"; TheNewAmerican.com; NYTimes.com; Congress.gov; CivilWar.org; TaxHistory.org; HistoryLink.org; U.S. Library of Congress LOC.gov); Mark Wilson "The Business of the Civil War"; Senate.gov/ArtAndHistory; U.S. Dept. of Commerce Bicentennial Edition Historical Statistics of the United States; IRS.gov; The U.S. Constitution; NPR.org; TaxAnalysts.com*

Chapter 8

The Income Tax Repealed in 1872

See? Income Taxes Won't Last Forever

"The income tax has been unpopular from the moment of its enactment. It has been tolerated just as various other obnoxious taxes were tolerated because it was one of the inevitable burdens entailed upon us by a great war. We have reached the time when the income tax can be no further defended [it] is not worth its cost.."

- New York Times
January 19, 1871

The prior two chapters summarized the first income tax plan of 1861, the updated law of 1862, and then the expanded (and more complex) tax system of 1864. It's interesting that once the Civil War concluded, the federal income tax was not immediately rescinded but was kept in place. Even if one argued that there was a need to keep it for two additional years (1866 and 1867) in order to pay down outstanding war-related expenses and military debts, the logic of recognizing this new extra source of federal revenue had served its purpose, and should have prompted the Congress to abolish the

76

income tax, treating it as it was originally intended – as a temporary measure linked directly to the required expenses of the Civil War. But the government had become very comfortable siphoning money from private individuals and businesses, and like all addicts, it had now become dependent on the regular 'fix' of collecting income tax revenues, and then legislating new ways to spend those funds.

Origin. By the end of 1867, there was widespread opposition to the income tax remaining in place, especially now that the war was over and the Union had been saved. Tariffs and excise taxes had covered the basic costs of government for nearly 75 years prior to the 1861-1862 laws with no need for additional taxation on incomes. The compromise was reached where Congress dramatically cut tax rates on both business and personal earnings, but did not go so far as to rescind what had originally been thought of as a provisional income tax. Congress did amend the 1864 tax code into the first *flat tax,* with the initial tax-free exemption raised to $1,000 and everything else above that taxed at 5 percent. But with the rate now flattened out and the exemption raised, the Senate made several attempts to make the income tax permanent. Their debates are well documented and prove conclusively that the original income tax was in fact temporary, both in its initial intent AND its structure. Not only have we reviewed how the founders clearly understood an income tax to be an invasion of personal property and a threat to individual liberty, but the overwhelming evidence from the public records of 1861 demonstrates such a *direct* tax was conceived for one purpose alone – to *temporarily* cover the additional expenses of the Union's war with the secessionists. And once that endeavor was completed, there would be no need for personal and business income taxes to remain in place. One notable 1867 editorial from the *New York Times* referenced income taxes as: "no businessman could pass the day without suffering from those burdens".

During the first few post-Civil War years (1865-1868) of very spirited discourse, the Supreme Court initially gave its unanimous support to making the original temporary tax permanent. Then the debate became somewhat biased during 1866 when the U.S. Treasury took in just over $310 million in taxes – the highest total in the 90 years since declaring independence from Britain – in fact federal revenues were not that high again for another 45 years until 1911. It was no doubt hard for politicians to seriously consider discontinuing the income tax while government coffers were bursting with all that cash. However, by the beginning of 1868, the Court's justices were regularly responding to a wide range of legal challenges regarding the validity of "that old Civil War income tax" impacting business dividends, real estate, and inheritances (the "death tax" will be covered in full detail in Chapter 17) – so the question always remained: *does the Constitution allow direct taxation of its citizens?*

Rationale. As the House and Senate continued their debates, the clock was actually ticking on those original statutes from 1861 1862, because the wording in those laws had actually been quite specific, as at least four of the higher excise taxes, along with the ιew income tax, had language referring that the law shall be in force ιntil 1870 and no longer. So as 1868 turned into 1869, and then ʰe new year had lawmakers reviewing the wording "1870 and no ɔnger", the Congressional delegations were dealing with another imeframe for the income tax, namely, that the amended 1864 law ιad an inferred maximum extension of eight years ("two White House erms") until 1872. Senate documents and a speech by President ᴧndrew Johnson (after Lincoln's assassination, his VP became the 7th president – from 1865 to 1869) included strong arguments in avor of allowing the law to expire. The *New York Tribune* noted the *ꞁirect* income tax was "unnecessary, unfair, the most odious, ᵉxatious, inquisitorial, and unequal of all our taxes, in its ɔllections, apparatus, and methods". The U.S. Archives shows that ιst three states (New York, Pennsylvania, Massachusetts) accounted ɔr over 60 percent of all income tax revenues collected, so there was strong sentiment that the 1864 tax law was inherently imbalanced ᶜcross all taxpayers nationwide. On February 14, 1872 (Valentine's ꞁay) the House of Representatives introduced bill "*HR-1537 To ꞁeduce Existing Taxes (the 42nd Congress)*" and the eventual vote was ᵛverwhelming to not take any steps to renew the *Internal Revenue Act ꞡ 1864,* but simply allow it to expire (I'm applauding as I type this).

Madness. One can only imagine the strong positive economic ⁿpact this news had on the New York Stock Exchange, as well as ᵐmall businesses, households, and individuals. But like some sort of ᵗreless, steadfast boxer in the ring that just won't go down and stay

79

down, the supporters of the permanent income tax went along witl the 1872 repeal because they had their sights set on crafting ai entirely new and greatly expanded income tax bill, and did not wan to simply augment or extend the most recent 1864 law. Much like child who is given a weekly allowance (for no work), and then i shocked and cannot imagine those cash payments being halted politicians had experienced a robust pipeline of tax funds to spen on all kinds of government programs, and could not fathom lif without that money. The 10-year expansion of federal spending ha acclimated Congress to an entirely new power structure based oi financial resources under its control, and Washington, D.C. ha already fallen prey to lobbyists representing various constituents.

Senators and members of the House had seen the positiv effects of these federal taxes appropriated to their home states an Congressional districts – in the forms of construction contracts fo civic projects, manufacturing and production output to mee government contract orders for various military support goods, join federal and private sector waterways, along with scores of new job created for voters who put them – and kept them – in elected publi office. The income tax represented a huge financial windfall to th federal government once the war was over, and the thought c shutting off those funds was contrary to the typical bureaucrati mindset of that day (not unlike today's politicians). But that ver same public sentiment was collectively heard loud and clear, fror the House to the Senate as well as the president's office – as peopl nderstood the *direct* income tax was in fact highly intrusive into the ves of private citizens, and carried the negative effects of wasting me and resources planning business and personal activities around 1e burdensome reporting-accounting and payment of the tax.

For the remainder of the 1870s and then throughout the very rosperous 1880s, the income tax had been, in most people's minds, elegated to a thing of the past – a vestige from a bygone era when xtraordinary measures were needed to help keep the Union together. ut for most politicians, the income tax was an experiment that had orked fairly well in its initial trials, and represented a potentially uge new permanent source of government revenue. The problem as finding the right time with the right issues through which to re-ntroduce it – not only to replenish the U.S. Treasury, but also to use as a political tool to penalize successful business profitability and xpansion, while advancing a misguided and errant form of social istice. The next chapter looks at the income tax comeback of 1894.

esearch and analysis sources include: *TaxFoundation.org; ncyclopedia.com; Politiact.com; Federal-Tax-Rates.InsideGov.com; heNewAmerican.com; Bradford Tax Institute; U.S. Library of Congress OC.gov); Senate.gov/ArtAndHistory; U.S. Dept. of Commerce istorical Statistics of the United States; CivilWar.org; IRS.gov; The U.S. onstitution;Archives.gov; Mises.org*

Chapter 9

The Income Tax of 1894

Just Kidding . . . It's Back

*"Collecting more taxes than is absolutely
necessary is legalized robbery."*

- Calvin Coolidge
President, 1923-1929

Now that Congress had moved, in 1872, to formally allow th

prior income tax to expire, the rest of the 1870s and all of the 1880

proved to be a period of strong economic expansion, significant jo

creation, and prosperity for business owners and individuals alike

Imagine that. Without that tax, private enterprise saw immediat

gains in profits, creating new capital for investment into facilitie

equipment, machinery, and product development, plus advances i

transportation and energy infrastructure such as railroads, canal

and coal production, all with significant job creation. The feder

government was again funded primarily by tariffs and excise taxes

even as it had been for the 75 years from the final ratifying of th

Constitution in 1789, up to the *Revenue Act* of 1862. It's worth noting that the fears of how government would survive without the income tax were quickly allayed as the booming economy generated a huge surge in tariff revenues on foreign trade imports and exports, as well as excise taxes on sin and luxury goods, because more and more people had greater amounts of discretionary income to spend on alcohol, billiard tables, tobacco, jewelry, carriages, and boats. Yes, the U.S. was back to paying all the costs of the federal government and the common defense quite well with *indirect* taxes alone.

Origin. This upbeat post-Civil War era in America was characterized by groundbreaking innovations, creativity, and new inventions that transformed the nation into a formidable industrial power. The southern states reconstruction transformed that region from plantations with highly concentrated wealth among elitist, aristocratic landowners, into smaller parcels of land for tenant farming and sharecropping. In contrast, the northern states built a vibrant and dominating industrial infrastructure, focused on heavy manufacturing, coal and steel production, railroad transportation development and expansion, along with major banking, finance, and insurance companies. The new factories, shipping ports, railroad yards, canal waterways, mines, and financial sectors created one of the strongest periods of job creation in American history, as literally millions of former farmers moved from the countryside into the cities in pursuit of new skills and professions in large-scale industries – as well as the financial and communications networks to support them.

U.S. Gross Domestic Product (GDP) was $8 billion at the time the income tax expired in 1872, generated throughout a population of almost 41 million people. By 1880, GDP had grown to just over $10.5 billion. In 1885 it was $11.7 billion, and at the end of 1880s it was $14 billion (population at 61 million) – up at a steady pace of 4 percent annual growth for essentially two full decades. It was unprecedented sustained economic expansion. By the mid-1880s, Andrew Carnegie had introduced steel manufacturing innovations that lowered costs and shortened production times, while greatly improving the quality and strength of the finished output. John Rockefeller took a fledgling Cleveland refinery and built it into the Standard Oil Company, aggregating some 90 percent of America's pipelines and refineries. Cornelius Vanderbilt, Collis Huntington, Edward Harriman, and James Hill masterminded the incredible expansion and modernization of the railroads for both commercial and personal transportation – including putting their capital and vision together to build the transcontinental railroad (perhaps you are, like me, a big fan of the television series *Hell On Wheels*).

John Pierpont Morgan organized a sophisticated financial products-services infrastructure that included banks in London and New York, making investment capital available to all kinds of 1880s inventors and designers, including funding all of Thomas Edison's development of commercial electricity for the masses, as well as his remarkable phonographic recording device. Morgan also facilitated investors to back George Eastman's revolutionary Kodak flexible

10tographic rolled film and camera, Henry Seeley's electric iron, 0hn Loud's self-contained ballpoint pen, and the rapid national :pansion of John Pemberton's carbonated drink, Coca-Cola.

At the start of the 1890s it was the Victorian Era in England, 1d life in America had known 18 consecutive years of mostly osperity and growth. The 1880s industrialists had created massive :w wealth throughout the U.S. economy, but some concerns were :ing expressed by liberal politicians that commercial and societal equities were being fostered with the emergence of the new middle ass and the super rich, while the rest of the population was ipposedly being left out of all this new prosperity. During the esidential election of 1892, the lead Democrat – Grover Cleveland – ntinuously made speeches about the divide in the economic isses of Americans, and tried to raise awareness of the purported equities and unfairness of the tariff and excise tax systems that nded the federal government, believing it put too much of a burden lower income workers and the poor, and did not spread tax yments equally among the population – especially the rich and the rgest businesses. And while there was no income tax on the profits the big industrial companies or the earnings of the wealthy men 10 founded and managed them, the railroads, steel mills, coal ines, and shipping yards were in fact paying huge proportions of e tariffs and excise taxes that funded the federal government. But eveland won the election by stirring up passionate sentiment that 0mething has to be done to correct the course of this once great

nation" (once great? – wait, it was in fact great right at the very tin
he was running for office, and would have no doubt remained ;
without his new plan for federal intervention into the private sector)

With the administration of William Henry Harrison windi
down in 1892, the Reading Railroad (Pennsylvania) went into wh
today would be called Chapter-11 bankruptcy reorganization, ar
this had a devastating negative ripple effect on dozens of large banl
and hundreds of businesses that depended on that Reading compar
This "Panic of 1893" impacted the European banks to withdraw the
funds from American banks, the stock markets in both New Yo
and London crashed, and then millions of average citizens rushe
the banks to get their money out before it was gone for good. Whe
President Cleveland took the oath of office in February 1893, U.
Gross National Product (total income) was already beginning its fre
fall into contraction, and after two consecutive fiscal quarters
declining GNP of more than ten percent, and with four million peop
having lost their jobs, it was officially a severe recession, and wou
become known as "The Depression of 1893".

Rationale. By the summer of 1894, it had been 22 years sin
the abolition of the *direct* income tax; however, President Clevelar
and the Congress agreed that the extraordinary events in the U.
economy merited immediate (and equally extraordinary) legislati
action to fix this newly exasperated "great divide" that was perceiv
between the rich and poor. Two Democrat colleagues of t
president (one from West Virginia and the other from Marylan

rafted their *Wilson-Gorman Tariff Act* with the intention of greatly reducing and eliminating trade tariffs to spur the economy out of the depression. But the new law would also reinstate the *direct* income tax to make up for those lower (and lost) tariff revenues. Leave it to an economic crisis to be the rallying point for taxing the rich more to create greater fairness and equality. This was the same mentality that developed President Obama's misguided American Recovery and Reinvestment Act of 2009 – a massive $831 billion government tax-and-spend "stimulus" that was supposed to kick-start the economy out of recession into fast-growth GDP and robust job creation. Instead, the last seven years have averaged only 2 percent annual increases in GDP, while over 90 million workers have left the U.S. labor pool, and only about 4.5 million net new jobs have been added after accounting for the nearly 11 million jobs lost to the recession.

Reviewing the various speeches, newspaper articles, and select congressional documents of that day, they have the same verbiage (and even the similar tone) of the contemporary broken-record liberal mantra – that the "one percent" are not paying their fair share, all economic growth is overly concentrated among the already wealthy, gains in wages and incomes aren't being equally distributed, and the income tax code should be used to facilitate a more fair manner of wealth redistribution from the rich to the poor. This pervasive form of illogical thinking continues to this day, maintaining that America's already dysfunctional IRS tax code must be further expanded to try and legislate, orchestrate, and *manipulate* economic equality.

Madness. This new income tax of 1894 was a basic *flat tax* of two percent on incomes over $4,000 (the equivalent of $105,000 in 2016 terms), so it would only be paid by less than 10 percent of all Americans. Tariffs on things like imported wool, coal, lumber, and iron ore were completely eliminated, making these foreign goods very competitively priced compared to the same domestically produced goods, and this was hotly contested by American manufacturing companies. So the Senate version of the House bill folded in more than 500 amendments and earmarks that actually *increased* other tariffs as part of a compromise plea-bargain with various businesses that would be hit hardest by reduced or eliminated foreign duties. This infuriated Cleveland that the final bill was not concise in its format, so he would not officially sign the bill into law; however, he did allow the new tariff structure and the *direct* income tax to go into effect. The thinking was that the reduced and eliminated trade tariffs would spark massive economic growth, and when the wealthy 1-in-10 saw their earnings grow, they would simply send in a small portion of those as income tax to the U.S. Treasury, and this would make up for the projected tariff revenue shortfall.

The *New York Times* then reported on January 30, 1895 "Democrats More Hopeful" even though in the end, the new law was another round of political maneuvering along strict party lines, where influential senior Democrat lawmakers in the industrial eastern and northern states "preferred to take the income tax – odious as it is and unpopular as it is bound to be with their constituents" rather

ιan send *Wilson-Gorman* down to defeat. The income tax was back
n the books, but this started a whole new round of legal challenges
ɔ its economic value, process, and (again) constitutionality. Less
ιan a year after it went into effect, the Supreme Court decided that
ertain portions of the *Tariff Act* were in fact unconstitutional. This
ack-and-forth debate would last another twenty years until in 1913
ʼhen an entirely new round of arguments and perspectives came
ɔgether to make *direct* income taxes permanently part of American
fe by amending the U.S. Constitution. (See the following chapter.)

esearch and analysis sources include: *TaxFoundation.org;
ʼncyclopedia.com; TaxHistory.org; Politiact.com; U-S-History.com;
ederal-Tax-Rates.InsideGov.com; TheNewAmerican.com; Bradford Tax
ιstitute; OurDocuments.org; U.S. Library of Congress (LOC.gov);
enate.gov/ArtAndHistory; U.S. Dept. of Commerce Historical Statistics
f the United States; IRS.gov; The U.S. Constitution; WSJ.com*

Chapter 10

The 16ᵗʰ Amendment of 1913

Really? Now It's In The Constitution

"Government's view of the economy can be summed up in a few short phrases: if it moves tax it, if it keeps moving regulate it; and if it stops moving – subsidize it."

- Ronald Reagan
President, 1981-1989

Origin. Even as it had been roughly 20 years since the repea of the earlier income tax from 1872 until the second-round version (Wilson-Gorman* in 1894, it would be almost another 20 years unt the next milestone in America's misguided history of taxes, when i 1913 the *Underwood-Simmons Tariff Act* again would cloak *dire* income tax legislation under the guise of "fixing and updating" trac tariffs, much like the customs duties bill two decades earlier. Th 1894 income tax was struck down by the U.S. Supreme Court in th 1895 landmark case of *Pollock vs. Farmers' Loan & Trust Compan* when the justices' decision rang clear that "this is a *direct* tax as pe rticle I, Section 9 of the Constitution, so it must then be levied in

roportion to the U.S. Census or Enumeration". Yet it was, of course,

ot assigned or collected in that proportional manner. With the

ncome tax collected solely on the basis of one's specific personal or

usiness income (and not based upon population), it was found to be

n "unapportioned direct tax" and therefore unconstitutional.

For the next 16 years (from 1895-1911), this ruling galvanized

onservative Republicans opposed to reviving the 1894 income tax,

hile rallying liberal Democrats to push for the federal income tax to

ecome permanent. The 1896 presidential election divided the

ation on this very issue, as Republican William McKinley defeated

emocrat William Jennings Bryan just 51-47 percent in the popular

ote, winning 23 of the 45 states (271-176 in electoral votes). The win

as interpreted as American voters wanting the income tax to be

voked, and much greater support for domestic manufacturing and

roducts. This shift to stricter trade tariffs and protectionism for

merican industry trumped the income tax, and customs duties were

nce again the number one source of the government's revenue. So

e federal income tax lay dormant for the next four years. McKinley

on a rematch with Bryan in the 1990 election, and had much

ronger support with a 52-45 percent majority, while winning 28 of

5 states (good for a stronger 292-155 electoral college victory). This

me McKinley's vice-president was New York Governor and Spanish-

merican War hero (for his duty in Cuba), Teddy Roosevelt – who

as also considered somewhat progressive in his political views.

91

William McKinley
(1897 – 1901)

Teddy Roosevelt
(1901 – 1909)

William Howard Taft
(1909 – 1913)

But when President McKinley was assassinated in September 190

Roosevelt finished the remaining 3 years as president, maintainir

strong conservative policies on tariffs, trade, and the economy. F

then won the 1904 election by a landslide (336-140) as he continue

to downplay any need for a federal income tax. He was followed t

the more conservative Republican William Howard Taft (1909-1913

who openly campaigned that he was not opposed to an income ta

and then stated during his inaugural address that a *direct* tax cou

be constitutionally permissible and maybe even desirable under tl

extraordinary circumstances of dire need. That caveat of "dire nee

allowed Taft to appear open to the ideas presented by Democrat

while still keeping the income tax from new or pending legislation.

 Rationale. These four presidential terms (16 years) ha

rebuffed any advances from the liberal politicians in the House ar

Senate to put different structures into the 1894 income tax so that ɔuld be revived. But by the election of 1912, the national debate ad swung back to the purported inequalities and unfairness of the ealthy not being willing to pay their "fair share" on those wealthy arnings, and Democrat Woodrow Wilson was elected while getting ɔly 41 percent of the vote in a 4-man race, but wining 40 of the 48 ates. His very first agenda item – just a month after being sworn in

**President Woodrow Wilson
(1913 – 1921)**

ɔ March 4th of 1913 – was to champion the *Underwood-Simmons ariff Act* to the American people. The Democrats were successful in aming the accompanying income tax as something all conservatives ɔould agree to, because it would clearly demonstrate support and ssistance for America's lower-wage earners and the poor. It was

93

also purported to be the best way to address the "growing divid« between the wealthy vs. "average people" by cutting or eliminatir virtually all tariffs, to bring in more foreign imported goods as a wɛ to help reduce prices for the essential products people buy every da It took just a modest six months of lawmaker debate, and in Octobɛ of 1913 the new law was passed. The U.S. once again had a feder; income tax – this time (they believed) it would become permanent.

The revised income tax was similarly packaged within whɛ appeared to be an import-export tariff law. Americans soon learne that they would be *directly* taxed based upon their specifi individual income levels. The main rate was one percent on earnin§ between $4,000 and $20,000 – then several graduated (higher) ratɛ at benchmarks as income went up, topped off by the maximum ra of six percent on every dollar earned over $500,000. The opposi page shows the newly revised 1913 individual income tax form wil the various levels of progressively higher marginal tax rates. It very interesting to note that our nation's founders of the late 170(argued strongly that if any *direct* income tax was ever adopted, thoɛ citizens with the highest incomes should pay the lowest tax rates (ɛ a monetary reward for their hard work, creativity, perseverance, ar industry), while the lowest earners should be the ones paying at tl highest rates (in order to provide economic incentive to better onesɛ take some additional investment or business risks, and be open pursuing enterprising opportunities that would have reasonab expectations for increasing one's personal lot in life).

94

The 1913 Income Tax Form

TO BE FILLED IN BY COLLECTOR.	Form 1040.	TO BE FILLED IN BY INTERNAL REVENUE BUREAU.

List. No. ....

.... District of ....

Date received ....

INCOME TAX.

THE PENALTY
FOR FAILURE TO HAVE THIS RETURN IN
THE HANDS OF THE COLLECTOR OF
INTERNAL REVENUE ON OR BEFORE
MARCH 1 IS $20 TO $1,000.
[SEE INSTRUCTIONS ON PAGE 4.]

File No. ....

Assessment List ....

Page .... Line ....

UNITED STATES INTERNAL REVENUE.

RETURN OF ANNUAL NET INCOME OF INDIVIDUALS.
(As provided by Act of Congress, approved October 3, 1913.)

RETURN OF NET INCOME RECEIVED OR ACCRUED DURING THE YEAR ENDED DECEMBER 31, 191 ....
(FOR THE YEAR 1913, FROM MARCH 1, TO DECEMBER 31.)

Filed by (or for) .... of ....
(Full name of individual.) (Street and No.)

in the City, Town, or Post Office of .... State of ....
(Fill in pages 2 and 3 before making entries below.)

		$
1.	GROSS INCOME (see page 2, line 12)	$
2.	GENERAL DEDUCTIONS (see page 3, line 7)	$
3.	NET INCOME	$

Deductions and exemptions allowed in computing income subject to the normal tax of 1 per cent.

4.	Dividends and net earnings received or accrued, of corporations, etc., subject to like tax. (See page 2, line 11) . . . $
5.	Amount of income on which the normal tax has been deducted and withheld at the source. (See page 2, line 9, column A)
6.	Specific exemption of $3,000 or $4,000, as the case may be. (See Instructions 3 and 19) . . . .

Total deductions and exemptions. (Items 4, 5, and 6) . . . . $

7. TAXABLE INCOME on which the normal tax of 1 per cent is to be calculated. (See Instruction 3) . $

8. When the net income shown above on line 3 exceeds $20,000, the additional tax thereon must be calculated as per schedule below:

					INCOME.	TAX.
1	per cent on amount over $20,000 and not exceeding $50,000 . .	$		$
2	"	"	50,000	"	"	75,000 .
3	"	"	75,000	"	"	100,000 .
4	"	"	100,000	"	"	250,000 .
5	"	"	250,000	"	"	500,000 .
6	"	"	500,000	. . . .

Total additional or super tax . . . . $

Total normal tax (1 per cent of amount entered on line 7) . . $

Total tax liability . . . . $

Table 10.1 summarizes the graduated tax rates of the 1913 tariff law. After the exemption from income taxes on the first $4,000 of earnings, the typical manufacturing factory worker, farmer, miner, agricultural laborer, rail- or dock-worker paid no tax, as their wages

Table 10.1
Personal Income Tax Rates – 1913

Marginal Tax Rate	Earnings Over	But Not Over
1%	- zero -	$ 20,000
2%	$ 20,000	$ 50,000
3%	$ 50,000	$ 75,000
4%	$ 75,000	$100,000
5%	$100,000	$250,000
6%	$250,000	$500,000
7%	$500,000	- no limit -

averaged between $3.50 and $5.68 per day. For the typical 300 days worked per year (adjusted for Sundays and holidays), average annual incomes were around $1,000 to $1,700. This put them well below that $4,000 exemption (the $3,000 baseline, plus the extra $1,000 for a married couple). For example, an assembly-line laborer making around $20 a week was at $1,000 annually and paid zero income tax. His foreman, making $50 a week ($2,500 for the year) also paid no income tax. The plant manager making $85 a week ($4,400 for the year) paid one percent ($4) on the $400 over the exemption ($1,400 he wasn't married). The materials buyer making $100 a week ($5,200

year) paid one percent on the $1,200 above the exemption, only
12 – while the regional sales manager who made $250 a week
13,000 a year) paid $90 in taxes, the same one percent on $9,000.
ne income tax was obviously aimed directly at the "wealthy"
ısiness owners, bankers, and industrialists, because the owner of
ıe factory who earned $300,000 would then pay income taxes at six
fferent (progressively higher) rates:

- One percent on the first $16,000   = $ 160
- Two percent on the next $30,000   = $ 600
- Three percent on the next $25,000   = $ 750
- Four percent on the next $25,000   = $ 1,000
- Five percent on the next $150,000   = $ 7,500
- Six percent on the final $50,000   = $ 3,000

       Total Taxable Income $296,000   = $13,010 Tax.

ıis worked out to a 4.39 percent effective tax rate, with $13,010 in
xes paid on $296,000 total taxable income (only the earnings above
ıe $4,000 exemption were taxed). Like its predecessors, this new
'rect tax would end up applying to only a very small portion of the
.S. population (around nine percent), bringing in a relatively low ten
ːrcent of all federal revenues in its first year – with the majority of
ɔvernment income coming from tariffs and domestic excise taxes.

     Republican lawmakers continued to be unconvinced about the
ɔnstitutionality of charging different rates for different incomes, and

argued instead for a single flat tax and either a lower, or ze: exemption that would remedy the troublesome *apportionment* issu across the population more equally. They ultimately agreed that tl tariff was actually not a tax, whereas they viewed the income tax be a form of 'economic class legislation' that would end up beir divisive for the overall republic. Once again, legal challenges we filed as to whether this tax was constitutional, with the main issu being revived from prior suits that dealt with the "unapportione issues of a *direct* income tax. The proposed new tariff regulations 1913 were again aimed at reducing or eliminating payments due on wide range of manufactured goods, with this new income te component added to compensate for the lost revenues on import ar export tariffs. Four years earlier, the *Payne-Aldrich Tariff Act* of 19(had moderately reduced some customs duties, but stopped short sweeping cuts that would help to make the case for a new income te as a "logical" (but misguided) way to make up the revenue shortfall.

The 1913 debate included liberal politicians and some ve progressive Republicans advocating for a dozen graduated tax rate between the $4,000 exemption and a top bracket of $1 million – wi Illinois House Republican Ira Copley actually proposing a 68 perce: tax on earnings "in excess of one million dollars". How and where (he come up with that outrageously high top rate? In contrast, Hen Cabot Lodge, the Senator from Massachusetts, argued the exemptic and tiers in the graduated higher tax rates "set different class apart [from one another] and says they are to be pillaged [as] the

98

roperty is confiscated". Right back at you, Wisconsin Senator
obert La Follette advocated an 11 percent top tax rate to finally
ddress "the national menace of [the] great accumulation of wealth".

**U.S. Senator Henry Cabot Lodge
(1893 – 1924)**

national menace? Some more moderate positions in the great tax
ebate of 1913 included Mississippi Senator John S. Williams who
ut forth this interesting perspective: "an honest man cannot make
ar upon great fortunes, per se, and I am not going to make this
iriff bill a panacea for all the inequalities of fortunes existing in this
ountry". He further opined about some future time period when

"the good day comes, the golden day, when there will [finally] be n taxes upon consumption at all". This was clearly a direct rebuke c the Republicans who wanted a simple flat tax for everyone, t eliminate the 'class' of the exemption and the higher graduated rate based on personal or business earnings. It was clearly understoo that garnering income taxes from U.S. citizens should not end u pitting Americans against one another due to their earning capacity savings, investments, land, and other wealth. The direct tax did i fact cut deeply into the very personal (and private) property c individuals, in essence penalizing those who had done well, whil rewarding those who had not with the opportunity to be tax-free provided one could keep income minimal. Quite a great disincentiv for creativity, innovation, and hard work.

Madness. The exact language from our Constitution state: *"No Capitation, or other direct, Tax shall be laid, Unless in Proportion t the Census of Enumeration herein before directed to be taken".* Th term 'capitation' comes from "capita" – used commonly when talkin about per-person economic numbers (*per capita spending* or *pe capita income).* The new tax law went into effect in October 1913 an immediately was challenged about its constitutionality due to thos graduated tax rates that "distinguish" between individuals, creatin de facto classes of individuals and businesses, rather than bein consistent with the capitation apportionment of a flat tax, where one size-fits-all without distinctions between taxpayers' earnings (relativ wealth). One notable tax case that went to the Supreme Court wa

Brushaber vs. The Union Pacific Railroad (1916), where the justices upheld the Underwood law because it "did not transcend the conception of taxation" and as such was not "a mere arbitrary abuse of power" by the federal government. But wait a minute! That makes no sense. The 1913 law DID discriminate among taxpayers, based entirely on their income capacity to pay the tax. The fine line in the debate shifted not from the inherent distinctions between taxpayers that did result from the law, to the law being equally applied to all without individual or group preference – the legal right now based on: "everyone has to pay" and not: "everyone pays at different rates".

The most glaring fact to comprehend is that the U.S. operated very well without a sustainable income tax for 125 years – from the Constitution in 1789, until the 16th Amendment in 1913 – and yet, in the 103 years we've had that income tax (along with the Federal Reserve, also launched in 1913), the federal debt has grown by 5,000 times! The next chapter introduces the Internal Revenue Service.

Research and analysis sources include: IRS.gov; Law.Cornell.edu; TaxFoundation.org; Bureau of Labor Statistics; Encyclopedia.com; The U.S. Constitution; Federal-Tax-Rates.InsideGov.com; National Bureau of Economic Research; History.House.gov; TheNewAmerican.com; Bradford Tax Institute; U.S. Library of Congress (LOC.gov); Government Publishing Office; ConstituionCenter.org; Senate.gov/ArtAndHistory; U.S. Dept. of Commerce Historical Statistics of the United States

Chapter 11

Meet The Internal Revenue Service

No, Really, This Is What They Do

> *"The IRS is like the mafia,*
> *they can take anything they want."*

> - Jerry Seinfeld
> American Comedian

Madness. This is the one chapter in the book where – unlik all the others – it makes perfect sense to start off with the 'madness and then get around to the 'origin' and 'rationale' afterward, becaus the Internal Revenue Service truly is a dysfunctional organization with illogical policies, and represents the epitome of governmen bureaucracy without limits. Think of this chapter as *my audit* of th IRS. And while Jerry Seinfeld's opening remark makes us all laugh herein lies the intense irony - because on the one hand, taxes hav become such an incredibly burdensome and invasive part c American life, the average citizen (myself included) has graduall become numb to the ridiculous rules, forms, and deadlines impose by this federal agency; yet on the other hand, everyone agrees tha e IRS is in fact very comical in its rules, forms, and deadlines. ìis is a timely reminder that the best suggested tagline-motto for e IRS in marketing its brand is: *"We have what it takes to take what* ›*u have"* – because that's literally how it functions.

Syndicated columnist Dave Barry quips: "We all try to ›operate fully with the IRS, because as citizens, we feel a strong ιtriotic duty not to go to jail". Celebrated humorist and author ırk Twain was a frustrated taxpayer during the 1861, 1862, and ¦64 original attempts at a federal income tax, as well as the 1872 peal, the 1894 revision, and he saw it struck down by the Supreme ›urt. His observation compared "a taxman to a taxidermist – with e only difference being that the taxidermist leaves the skin". Sam ɛmens died in 1910, three years before the *direct* income tax ›came a permanent amendment (fixture) to the U.S. Constitution. ›median Jay Leno offers this key piece of advice: "If you're worried ›out an IRS audit, then avoid what's called a red flag – for instance, you have any money left in your bank account after paying all your xes . . . THAT'S a red flag". *The Farmer's Almanac* provided this S commentary: "If Patrick Henry thought that taxation without presentation was bad, he should have seen how bad it is *with* presentation". Isn't it amazing that this institution can be so •spised (and ridiculed) by virtually every type of American, and yet e IRS continues functioning with a life unto itself – enforcing ιtutes, conducting audits, seizing assets, assessing penalties – all ìile putting fear in the hearts of both the wealthy and the not so.

Each year the non-profit *Tax Foundation* calculates out t**
"Tax Freedom Day" – the number of days the average American h**
to work in the new year to earn enough to cover all federal, state, ar
local taxes; ironically, it's typically around 110 days (almost on**
third of the year), or right about April 15th when federal income tax**
are due. How sad it is, that people have to work about 30 percent
the year just to pay their taxes. As such, consider this early 2(
century editorial from *The New* Yorker: "How appropriate it is th**
our month when taxes are due begins with 'April Fools Day' and en**
with plaintiff cries of 'May Day' ". Or consider how messed up t**
system is when one of my daughters gets all excited about receivi**
her tax refund in the mail, only to have me explain that it was alwa**
her money in the first place, and they're simply returning it. An**
was it intended or coincidence that the portion of this book about t**
IRS just happens to appear in Chapter-11 (the federal number for
common form of bankruptcy)? Each of these jokes and puns provi**
some comic relief from the harsh reality that the feder**
government's Treasury Department has a formal service, staffed wi**
tens of thousands of agents, dedicated to the sole pursuit of getti**
to our money for the government's spending purposes.

Origin. The previous chapter reviewed how the 1913 tariff l**
was the start of the modern-era tax code with the launch of t**
Bureau of Internal Revenue (BIR). The IRS website explains itself **
"originally a patronage system that later was replaced by care**
professional employees" (that's reassuring) – and this bureau of t**

J.S. Treasury is "one of the world's most efficient tax administrators, processing over 240 million tax returns in 2014, collecting $3.1 trillion in tax revenue". The IRS mission statement says it provides American taxpayers "top quality service by helping them understand and meet their tax responsibilities, and enforces the law with integrity and fairness to all". Before you find yourself standing at attention with your hand over your heart, there are hundreds of third-party commentaries that would of course take major issue with how this bureau of the Treasury actually does conduct itself.

First, in that 1913 inaugural year, the U.S. tax code was 400 pages. It's so intriguing to read of the incredulity and even outrage in newspapers, magazines, speeches, and editorials back in 1913 about why this federal plan required 400 pages to explain how to calculate and pay one's taxes. The *Harper's Weekly* magazine had originally published in 1876, the political cartoon on the next page depicting the federal income tax as a heavy, burdensome weight around the neck of the woman symbolizing peace, even as she is marked as the slave of liberty". This same illustration was reprinted numerous times in 1913, and often referred to as the clearest symbol of how free people become subjugated to the will of the government, when their liberty is encroached upon by a tax on their very livelihoods – personal income being recognized as the epitome of privacy, but now required to be publicly disclosed. Many argued that the most prosperous states provided shelter for those who had the highest incomes, so these top states would then be at a significan

disadvantage when the normal flow of capital for investments woul

now be reduced by individuals paying federal taxes on their personal income. And yet, by 1919, there were then eight states that had adopted their own income tax (in addition to the federal income tax) as the personal freedom of one's earnings was now coveted for taxes by two separate governments. Wait, really? Less than five years into the new federal income tax, and suddenly state legislatures and governors had already decided to head down the same pathway? This is moving then much deeper into . . .

More Madness. Would people from back then be able to even comprehend that today, the nonpartisan *TaxFoundation.org* reports the IRS tax code has hemorrhaged to more than nine million words (15 times the Bible) covering over 72,000 pages? The instructions to complete the 2-page IRS Form-1040 cover 114 pages and include 38 separate supplemental forms and schedules. That's why many people and businesses simply choose to NOT file. The *Tax Policy Institute* states "it's difficult to know how many people don't file an income tax return", but for 2015, TPI estimates that 43.5 percent of Americans (77 million households) did not pay federal income taxes. This is probably due to lower earnings levels, or people no longer being in the labor market making money. How many who don't file (but have enough income and should file), is hard to determine, but the IRS estimates that each year over two million individuals who should be paying taxes, choose to not file their returns.

If a person has any kind of W2 or 1099 income, is supposed to get a refund, but doesn't file a tax return, that money is forfeited after just three years. If the person owes taxes and doesn't file, it can take several years for the IRS to catch up, but when it does, its computers generate estimates of the unreported income and taxes due for those missing years, and a bill is sent out for those payments due – usually within 30 days of the notice. The back tax also has fines added, along with interest the IRS could have earned had the tax been paid on time. For example, owing $4,000 from 10 years ago would also include $2,000 in fines plus 120 months of compounded interest at several points over the banks' prime lending rate (3.25 percent from December 2000 until December 2015), tacking on an additional 50 percent to the combined $6,000 ($4,000 plus $2,000 in fines), for a grand total of around $9,000 due.

Failure to respond and make payments will then result in the IRS doing whatever it wants to collect the taxes, including: 1) freezing bank accounts (the taxpayer is denied access to the funds while the IRS decides how much money to take and when); 2) seizing personal assets like cars, homes, boats, jewelry, stocks (to be sold at public auctions to raise cash for back tax payments); and 3) garnishing wages (withholding tax directly from a paycheck before the person gets paid, because instead of going to prison, the IRS would rather have you continue working and paying back taxes). And while the *National Association of Tax Professionals* reports that the typical non-filer, once caught, is not very unlikely to go to prison, one *New Yorker* magazine cartoon shows a husband and wife watching television ith a man onscreen behind bars in jail, and a caption of her saying, Honey, that reminds me, did you file our tax return?"

The IRS Form-1040 federal tax filing is the responsibility of ach taxpayer to calculate, so how many people cheat on their ncome taxes? CNN reported in 2010 that the IRS Oversight Board urvey found that 13 percent said "cheating is acceptable", while 4 ercent stated they "cheat on their taxes as much as possible". The eal interesting results of the poll showed that 80 percent – four out f five taxpayers – said "it's never acceptable to cheat". (Ever wonder ow many of them *say* that, but still cheat on their taxes?) While 1ost cheating is intentional, tax analyst Mark Luscombe admits that large portion are simply "people who can't decipher the complicated 1x code; people can't figure it out so they just put down a number 1at seems pretty good to them". In fact, many tax advisors say that hen in doubt, make up a number or leave a section blank, and if 1e IRS sends back the recalculated return requesting an additional ayment due, then pay it and you save all the time and hassle of ying to figure it out on your own. And, if your return is not flagged nd you never hear back, then you not only saved the time and ggravation, but also the money.

More Rationale. The IRS today has an annual operations 1dget of $11 billion, employing over 100,000 agents stationed cross a national network of field offices, with the headquarters on onstitution (how fitting) Avenue in downtown Washington, D.C. By omparison, the U.S. Postal Service had 2014 revenue of $68 billion with 483,000 employees, and an operating loss of $5.5 billion – th record eighth straight year of losing money. Earlier in this chapter referenced from the IRS website its boast as "one of the world's mos efficient tax administrators", however, in January 2015, IR Commissioner John Koskinen announced that due to budge constraints and new training for enforcing Obamacare, the tim period to receive tax refunds would take several weeks longe taxpayer inquiries would be delayed up to a month, and wait times a the 1-800 helpline would average between 30 minutes and one hour

The IRS also decides which individuals and businesses t audit – some based upon random computer-selection, and other based upon intentional review. But in 2013 it was revealed that had specifically targeted conservative organizations (based upo name and/or reputation) for increased audit scrutiny, and then-IR Commissioner Lois Lerner had suddenly lost or "accidentally deletec tens of thousands of emails that likely contained evidence pertiner to the inquiry into her role in directing these audits. A memo fror Siri Buller (a tax specialist working for Lerner) outlined joir cooperation between the Department of Justice, the Federal Electio Committee, and the IRS to "prevent prohibited activity by thes [conservative] organizations". This was backed up by IRS files that i 2010 the agency posted special notices to its employees to be on th lookout for any "Tea Party" organizations applying for non-profit ta> exempt status. Lerner was called to testify, but she pleaded the Fift Amendment and the next day was placed on administrative leav

The following month (June 2013), she was paid a $42,000 bonus, even as the IRS admitted it used "inappropriate criteria" in targeting certain conservative groups. Two months later, Lerner retired with a full pension. The following May of 2014, she was held in contempt of Congress for refusing to testify, and the next month the IRS said it lost all of Lerner's emails from 2009-20011. But in December-2014, the Inspector General announced the 30,000 emails were recovered. The fiasco finally ended on March 31, 2015 when the Obama Administration's Justice Department announced that no criminal charges would be filed against Lerner. Another great job, IRS !

Economist Stephen Moore notes that "Washington demands full accountability and accuracy from [business and individual] tax filers, but its own tax collection department is the least accountable agency of government". In May-2015, *Forbes* reported that 61 percent of IRS employees who were caught willfully violating tax laws, were *not* fired, and some were actually promoted or received a bonus within one year of their infractions. The most common violations were overstating business expenses, habitually filing a late return, and taking first-time homebuyer tax credits, even when the agents didn't actually own a home.

Even More Madness. Various studies have now shown that the current ridiculous IRS tax compliance costs in: 1) lost time (work hours spent by individuals and businesses planning and preparing taxes), 2) direct payments for outside tax advice and preparation, and 3) materials costs of forms, software, printing, envelopes, and postage, total up to between $300–$450 billion annually – around twice the GDP of Peru. The Tax Foundation estimates individuals lose another 6.6 billion hours per year in wasted productivity at their jobs on tax compliance, representing another $200 billion. Together, these costs could generate a potential windfall of $650 billion in new funds for investment if a simpler, easier system was enacted – new private sector capital for R+D, improved infrastructure, modernizing plant-equipment, faster IT-networks, construction, and expanded markets – ALL resulting in strong private sector job creation.

Several years ago I was at the *Free Market Forum* and heard Daniel Hannan (British member of the European Parliament) deliver an inspiring address on the waste to viable enterprise of complying with increasing government regulation, noting that Europe does look west to America for leadership in how best to support capitalism and a thriving private sector by reducing and eliminating taxes that free up entrepreneurial innovation and creativity. From 2009-2013, the IRS taxed from private sector individuals and businesses on average 15 percent of the nation's total GDP, covering three different sources: 1) personal income taxes (49 percent of all taxes collected), 2) payroll taxes (41 percent), and 3) corporate taxes (10 percent). Think of that – about one in every seven dollars of the U.S. economy is confiscated by the IRS for wasteful government spending.

The IRS has had a 100-year run, including multiple scandals and even presidential administrations using the agency for political tactics against opponents. Elliott Roosevelt said of his father

Franklin: "[he] may have been the originator of the concept of employing the IRS as a weapon of political retribution". John F. Kennedy had the IRS intimidate Republican right-wing organizations in the now famous "Ideological Organizations Project", and the IRS illegally provided tax returns to the FBI for investigations into the NAACP, The Birch Society, the American Communist Party, as well as four IRS audits of Rev. Martin Luther King, Jr. and the Southern Christian Leadership Conference. The impeachment filed against Richard Nixon charged that he "endeavored to cause, in violation of the constitutional rights of citizens, income tax audits or other tax investigations to be initiated in a discriminatory manner". President Clinton allegedly ordered IRS audits of the Heritage Foundation and the NRA. And the Obama Administration was associated with the scandal involving the IRS' Lois Lerner targeting investigations of tax-exempt conservative organizations (most notably "Tea Party" groups) she referred to in her recovered emails as "evil and dishonest". The next chapter examines tax-specialist accountants and attorneys.

Research and analysis sources include: *TheTaxFoundation.org; IRS.gov; Encyclopedia.com; WSJ.com; Treasury.gov; Bradford Tax Institute; U.S. Library of Congress (LOC.gov); U.S. Dept. of Commerce Historical Statistics of the United States; DailyFinance.com; The U.S. Constitution; Reuters.com; Finance.Yahoo.com; USAToday.com; Tax-Freedom.com; NationalReview.com;TaxHistory.org*

Chapter 12

Meet the Tax Accountants and Tax Attorneys

No, Really, This Is What They Do

"The U.S. income tax created more criminals than any other single act of government."

- Barry Goldwater
5-Time U.S. Senator

Origin. The current tax code is so ridiculously complicated and convoluted that it requires highly-trained and formally educated tax "specialists" to guide individuals and businesses through the ever changing maze of legal write-offs, tax credits, exemptions, carry forward and carry back provisions, supplemental forms, depreciation schedules, depletion allowances, and other obscure deductions. The calculations from one's "gross income" to the eventual "taxable income" is a long and circuitous path that involves dozens (if not hundreds) of additions and subtractions to arrive at an exact amount on which the income tax will be paid. The IRS has purposefully designed the current line-up of more than 100 separate tax forms so hat there will be a unique place to insert numbers and calculate iterally every possible scenario of earnings and write-offs for ndividuals and businesses. These supplemental forms, schedules, and rates are then changed annually (or every few years) to reflect updates to tax provisions, regulations, and new legislation that Congress may decide is required. As such, it becomes virtually mpossible for the average person, household, or business owner to stay current with all of these. And in many cases, there is more than one legitimate way to depreciate, expense, or report figures within he IRS code, requiring very specific tax expertise to decide which is best for a given household or company. With hundreds of new IRS nstructional pages and provisions coming out each year, the tax code has grown to more than 70,000 pages – opening wide the door or highly educated accountants, attorneys, and estate professionals o create demand for their specific talents in all things tax-related.

Rationale. Some individuals and small businesses sit at the kitchen table with several file folders and boxes filled with all kinds of receipts, bank statements, and other hard-copy justifications of their income and deductions – along with a calculator, plenty of scratch paper, and the IRS instructions for Form 1040, and they fill out the paper copies of all the tax forms (picked up at the local post office, library, or PDFs from the IRS website), then mail in their tax returns with a check (or not, because they get a refund). Others sit down with their tax accountant and/or attorney months (if not the year) prior to the April 15th deadline, to formulate a comprehensive tax strategy and map out a plan for how to target and arrive at a certain income and line-up of deductions that will legally shelter a much of their money as possible from ending up at the Treasury Another group strolls into H & R Block (or similar national franchise and puts their trust in someone who just completed the 5-week ta preparation training program. The rest probably go online to Turb Tax, eTax, TaxAct, or similar and scroll through questions abou work, income, marital status, children, school tuition and loans charitable donations, housing, business – and at the end they pres the magic "ENTER" button to reveal whether they owe more money o are getting a refund. How sad is this current situation?

Madness. Today there are over 800 undergrad and graduat accounting programs at colleges and universities in the U.S. wit formal majors in "Tax Accounting". There are also more than thirt professional development online schools offering Master's degrees i "Taxation" (from online Southern New Hampshire, Keller at DeVr) and Taft – to Villanova, Rutgers, Bentley, and DePaul). In additior law schools offer the LLM (Latin Legum Magister) degree focuse solely on tax law. Boston University's program boasts "students wi not only master the fundamental concepts of tax law, but will als understand how complex tax issues are handled". Yes, the progra description states there are laws devoted entirely to taxes, and thes are (inherently) COMPLEX. The required courses include: Feder. Income Taxation I and II (sequential terms), Corporate Tax Law, Ta Practice and Procedure, and Partnership Tax Law. Electives cove

116

Estate and Gift Taxation, Inbound International Taxation, Taxation of Financial Products, and Legal Representations in Tax Law (to name just a few). That last course description notes, "You will demonstrate an expert knowledge of IRS tax policies, procedures, and practice, and be able to represent clients in tax controversies". It is well beyond logical reasoning that our misguided American tax system has digressed to such a condition of complexity and minutiae that accredited graduate tax and legal expertise is necessary to have any chance in dealing with the IRS and the 70,000 pages of code.

The American Institute of Certified Public Accountants (AICPA) governs the field of professional tax accounting. The exam for the designation of Certified Public Accountant (CPA) includes an entire section (of four total) dedicated to tax-related accounting laws and practices. The REG (regulations) section is 60 percent devoted to taxes and requires detailed knowledge about federal taxation for personal, corporate, and partnership returns. It also covers income, gift, and estate taxation, as well as special tax provisions for sole proprietorships, limited and general partnerships, the limited liability company (LLC), C-corporations, Subchapter-S corporations, trusts, joint ventures, and tax-exempt organizations. Preparation courses cover multiple tax accounting and legal topics. Individuals purchase preview-test courses, books, DVDs, and other study materials that cost between $750 and $3,000. Many attend in-person seminars costing $499 to $1,900 so they can learn test-taking strategies and walk through questions in practice versions of the full CPA exam.

A quick Google search of "tax attorney" brings up over 100,000 matches, and these range from high-end law firms that provide legal counsel about tax strategies for businesses, to various estate lawyers focused on wealthy individuals needing assistance with asset preservation, gifts, and inheritance taxes, to firms offering to assist taxpayers and small businesses with audits or problems with back taxes owed to the IRS. Top-end tax advice will be very expensive to hire accountants, attorneys, and estate tax planners. The range covers every size client and ability to pay. On the lower end of costs, many individuals and smaller companies with pending tax problems will hire firms such as Tax-Masters, Tax-Tiger, Optima Tax Relief, Stop IRS Debt, or Tax Defense Partners to review their IRS tax case and negotiate some form of settlement with the IRS to either reduce the total that is owed, or work out a payment plan to retire the outstanding liability of back taxes, penalties, and interest.

For the most recent data of 2012, the top 400 individual taxpayers in the U.S. had take-home pay averaging $336 million. If the majority of those funds had been salary or wages, the income tax payable would be just under 40 percent – about $134 million payable. However, most of their income was derived from sophisticated partnerships and high-end investment funds, as well as earnings accrued to complex family trusts and foreign shell corporations (which are often beyond the reach of American tax collectors). The highly paid accounting and legal tax-technicians who devise these complicated tax strategies typically work at large law firms, financial services companies, or investment banks, as well as a wide variety of seemingly obscure tax-planning boutiques. A "family office" (FO) sets up customized wealth management teams who focus specifically on U.S. taxpayers with hundreds of millions (even billions) of dollars in assets. These FOs have been around ever since the late 1890s (back to the trusts-era in steel, coal, railroads, banking, and shipping). The Rockefellers, Morgans, Gettys, and Fords started the practice, which regained popularity during the 1970s and 1980s, with tremendous proliferation in the last two decades as the number of mega-rich taxpayers, and the size of their estates, have increased to new highs.

A full-time team of tax professionals can leverage every legal loophole to minimize taxes on income and wealth, as they oversee investment strategies and philanthropy; however, tax planning is the core function. The specific tax techniques employed to minimize taxes are typically mind boggling in their complexity, like converting one type of income into another type that's taxed at a lower rate. One example involves using a Bermuda-based reinsurer (a firm that insures insurance companies), that turns around and invests into a hedge fund. That maneuver transforms profits (ordinary income) the government taxes at 39.6 percent, to long-term capital gains, which are taxed at roughly half that rate. It has the added advantage of allowing clients to defer taxes on this income indefinitely, so wealth grows more quickly. Among tax lawyers and accountants, "the best and brightest get a high from figuring out how to do tricky little deals," said Karen L. Hawkins, who until recently headed the IRS office that oversees tax practitioners. "Frankly, it is beyond our intellectual and resource capacity to catch [these]; the combination of cost and complexity make it very tough to locate and then prosecute these tax strategies". Whatever tax rates Congress sets, the effective rates actually paid by the mega-rich always tend to drop over time as they exploit their tax-specialist plans.

The reality is that tax accounting, tax law, and estate tax planning are big business in the U.S., with powerful lobbies focused on maintaining the long-term viability of the hundreds of thousands of accountants, lawyers, and estate management professionals whose entire value is dependent upon a convoluted, burdensome, and hard to understand tax code – without which, there is no need to employ tax specialists to assist individuals and businesses through the maze of regulations and requirements. "There's this notion that the wealthy use their money to buy politicians; more accurately, it's that they buy ... tax policy," said Jared Bernstein, a senior fellow at the left-leaning Center on Budget and Policy Priorities. "That's why these egregious loopholes exist, and why it's so hard to close them." The next chapter examines sales and income taxes at the state level.

Research and analysis sources include: *TaxFoundation.org; American Institute of Certified Public Accountants; Federal-Tax Rates.InsideGov.com; USNews.com; CNN.com; Bradford Tax Institute, TaxAnalysts.com; Law-Schools.StartClass.com; GradSchool.com, IRS.gov; Time.com; WSJ.com; Grad-Schools.USNews.com*

Chapter 13

State Sales And Income Taxes

Tax Every Purchase, Plus Your Income Again

"Why does a slight tax increase cost you two hundred dollars, and a substantial tax cut save you thirty cents."

- Peg Bracken
American Humorist

Origin. Earlier chapters reviewed how import-export tariffs and domestic excise taxes were the preferred *ad valorem* form of raising funds for government without specifically designating personal incomes for the *direct* tax. As individual states expanded their own government bureaucracies and social programs, it became evident they needed to devise their own plans for revenue funding, so they opted first for a statewide sales tax (indirect) on virtually all purchases made within their borders. It seemed to be "fair" and sought to spread the tax burden across all individuals, households, and businesses based upon regular purchases of goods and services. Forty-five states and the District of Columbia now have a tax on retail sales. The rates also include several add-on portions (surtaxes) that increase the baseline rate levied for specific counties and local municipalities on unique voter-approved ballot initiatives for certain spending, making the combined sales tax rate typically between 5 percent and 7 percent. Table 13.1 shows the ten highest state sale taxes in the U.S. Only four states don't have a sales tax: Oregon, New Hampshire, Montana, and Delaware.

Table 13.2

TOP-10 STATE SALES TAXES - 2014
Including Average Local Surtaxes

Tennessee	9.45%
Arkansas	9.19%
Louisiana	8.89%
Washington	8.88%
Oklahoma	8.72%
Alabama	8.51%
New York	8.47%
California	8.41%
Arizona	8.17%
Illinois	8.16%

Source: State Tax Policy, TaxFoundation.org

The negative impact of high sales taxes is very clear, as imposes additional costs to the prices for virtually all durable good purchases like: automobiles, motorcycles, home appliances, vacatio and recreational vehicles, trucks, boats, furniture, electronics, an virtually every type of home improvement outlay. The impact migh

ot seem that big on a $20 purchase at the local drug store (an extra
$1.64 here in Santa Barbara); however, buying a new washer-dryer
at the sale price of $999 results in another $82 to cover the sales tax
– and that new $28,000 automobile adds on $2,300 in state sales tax.
Millions of daily purchases statewide really do add up to a huge
source of revenue, typically budgeted for the state's outlays of: public
education, health and human services, parks and natural resources,
and criminal corrections and rehabilitation. Granted, state sales
taxes are not part of the federal taxing machine, but they do present
an additional layer of government confiscation of private sector
income, as vendors are responsible to pay the sales tax on purchases
of their goods and services sold. The key issue should not be finding
more private sector activities to tax, but limiting the over-spending at
all levels of federal, state, and local governments.

With the adoption of the 16th Amendment, many states quickly
moved to implement *direct* income tax plans for their own residents.
Within just six years of the new federal income tax law, Mississippi
and Wisconsin (1913), Oklahoma (1915), Virginia and Massachusetts
(1916), Delaware and Missouri (1917), as well as New York and North
Dakota (1919) had put in place their own state income taxes. By the
Great Depression of the 1930s, another 18 states had added this tax.
Today, 43 states and the District of Columbia impose state income
taxes on top of the federal IRS income tax. Only seven states don't
have an income tax: Washington, Wyoming, Nevada, Texas, Florida,
South Dakota, and Alaska (started in 1949, but repealed it in 1979).

New Hampshire and Tennessee impose an income tax only on stock dividends and interest income, but not on typical salaries and wages. Table 13.2 shows the ten highest state income taxes.

Table 13.2

TOP-10 STATE INCOME TAXES

Hawai'i	11.00%
Oregon	11.00%
California	10.30%
Iowa	8.98%
New Jersey	8.97%
New York	8.97%
Vermont	8.97%
Maine	8.50%
D.C.	8.50%
Minnesota	7.85%

Source: Forbes, November-2010

Having lived in southern California for 32 years, it is quite alarming to compare the prior two tables and find that only New York (8.97 and 8.47 percent) and my state (10.3 and 11.3 percent) show up on both Top-10 lists regarding the highest state sales taxes AND the highest state income taxes in the nation. Probably the only thing worse that being on both lists is living and working in New York City where the New York Department of Taxation and Finance has a city income tax for residents of the five boroughs: Manhattan, Brooklyn, Queens, The Bronx, and Staten Island. On average, that rate add about another 6 percent on top of the federal-IRS and New York state income taxes due each year. Ouch! It's hard to imagine coming up on April 15th every year, and having to complete such a debilitating triad of federal, state, and city income tax forms. And finally, there's the issue of states trying to figure out how to tax the income of persons whose business has them living in one state, while working a significant time in another state (or states). If your residence is in New Jersey, but you work full-time in Manhattan, is your city income subject to that additional tax? Many states use the "first day" rule, that if you earn income there even for one day, you owe that state income tax. Some have grace periods of two weeks up to two months, after which you'll owe that other state income tax. Others could care less about your time in their state, and assess the income tax based solely on meeting a minimum threshold of earnings. No matter how you look at it, the states (like the federal government) have become used to the sales tax and income tax revenues, and are not likely to reduce rates or agree to a national standard on taxing "state" income anytime soon. The next chapter examines capital gains taxes.

Research and analysis sources include: *TaxFoundation.org; Encyclopedia.com; BankRate.com; Federal-Tax-Rates.InsideGov.com; TheNewAmerican.com; TaxPolicyCenter.org; Bradford Tax Institute; U.S. Library of Congress (LOC.gov); Kipplinger.com; IRS.gov; The U.S. Constitution; Forbes.com; WSJ.com; Investopedia.com*

Chapter 14

Payroll Taxes

FICA And More Skimming Off The Top

"My last paycheck was for zero dollars, so I asked the accounting office, who said the new payroll tax laws are so confusing, they decided to play it safe and withhold everything."

- David Brenner
American Comedian

Origin. The modern payroll tax got started when the 1864 version of the *direct* income tax included the provision for employers to withhold anticipated taxes in weekly or monthly increments of the total that would eventually be due for the year. This "pay-as-you-go" (also called "pay-as-your-earn") method secured a regular monthly and quarterly revenue stream for the federal government, rather than collecting taxes just once or twice a year. For 70 years the payroll tax was simply each worker pre-paying their own income taxes that would be due at year-end. Payroll taxes today, however, include deductions for mandatory federal entitlement spending programs

126

he first is Social Security – started in 1935 to provide a government
uaranteed retirement income, disability income, and a survivor's
eath benefit. The second is Medicare, started in 1965 when
resident Lyndon Johnson added it to the payroll tax to provide
ealthcare for the elderly. Some states also have a third deduction
or their own state disability plans. The chart below shows Social
ecurity consuming half of government mandatory spending
nandatory is 65 percent of the 2016 federal budget) – the largest
utlay in the total federal budget, surpassing even defense spending.

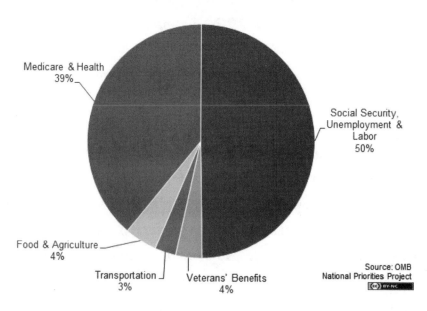

**President's Proposed
Mandatory Spending**
(Fiscal Year 2015)

Medicare & Health 39%

Social Security, Unemployment & Labor 50%

Food & Agriculture 4%

Transportation 3%

Veterans' Benefits 4%

Source: OMB
National Priorities Project

Payroll taxes show up on a person's paycheck stub under th label of "FICA" (*Federal Insurance Contributions Act*), with 6.2 percer of wages (up to the maximum earnings of $118,500) going to Socia Security, plus 1.45 percent for Medicare. The employee pays 7.6 percent, and the employer matches that, so the combined FICA i 15.3 percent of wages (12.4 percent Social Security plus 2.9 percer Medicare). Here in my state, employees also have 9/10ths of on percent deducted for California State Disability Insurance (CA-SDI For the self-employed, that total 15.3 percent payroll tax is pai entirely by the individual on IRS Form-SE. A California employe making $75,000 a year working for a company will have $6,413 i deductions for Social Security, Medicare, and CA-SDI – while a sel employed person with the same pre-tax income (after busines expenses) will be assessed $12,150 for these three payroll taxes.

Rationale. Social Security was launched to *"give som measure of protection to the average citizen, and to his family, again the loss of a job, and against poverty-ridden old age"* (excerpt from speech by Franklin Roosevelt on August 14, 1935). Many Americar believe their FICA taxes are put into their own "personal" Socia Security account and that earns interest during their working caree and is then ultimately released to them upon retirement – like 401k, 403b, or IRA. This is not the case. FICA taxes are collected an then paid out right away as benefits through the Social Securi Administration (SSA) for retirement income, disability income, ar death benefits to survivors. As long as there are enough peop paying in to cover benefits going out, it can remain viable. The initial math in 1937 was actually quite simple. Around 159 workers would pay one percent of their wages (up to $3,000) and their employers would match one percent, and this two percent total easily covered the benefits to ONE retiree – a lump sum pay-out at age 65. In 1940, retirees began receiving benefits on a monthly basis rather than a lump sum, and the ratio of workers paying in compared to workers receiving benefits dropped from 159:1 to 42:1 by 1945.

Then, five years after WWII ended the ratio dropped to 16:1. Fifteen years later in 1960 it was down to only 5:1, then 3.2-to-1 in 1980 – but still operating with an annual surplus (more funds paid in than benefits paid out). You might remember the 1994 Republican House and Senate "contract with America" that worked closely with President Clinton to cut spending, reduce social services pay-outs (e.g.: the welfare-to-work initiative), and balance the federal budget (there were huge federal tax windfalls collected in the dot.com era). Together these created a surplus in the Social Security trust fund, and helped bump the ratio a bit higher to 3.4-to-1 in 2000.

Madness. The SSA projects that the current 12 percent of the U.S. population over 65 will almost double to 23 percent by 2080. The 2016 ratio is now 2.7-to-1 and will hit 2:1 in about 20 years. An interesting September-2014 study published by *Sciencexpress* noted life expectancy in 1950 was 68 years, with 16 workers supporting one retiree; but today people live to 78, with less than 3 workers supporting one retiree – and that ratio is projected to drop to under

2:1 by the middle of this century, as life expectancy hits 82. There have been three main proposals to address the madness of this unsustainable public service. The first is to push the retirement age back, delaying the start of paying out benefits to retirees. The SSA amendments of 1983 "phased in a gradual increase in the age for collecting full benefits – from 65 to 67 over a 22-year period". Today several polls show that Americans are in favor of pushing the retirement age to 70, as many people now work all throughout their 60s. The second is to increase the payroll tax – referred to as "adjusting the cap" – a plan President Obama has called for many times (October 2008 campaign video), so that "people like myself are paying a little bit more" (appearing November 2007 on *Meet The Press*), by "not limiting the payroll tax to a ceiling, but taxing all income without a maximum limit" (September 2007 Op-Ed in *Quad City Times,* Iowa). And while these first two might buy some more time in the short run, the reality for the long-term is that the third option has to happen, where Social Security must ultimately be restructured, because the original 159:1 ratio is approaching 2:1. This would shift retirement benefits from being paid by current workers' payroll taxes, to a "personal" account that is invested over time (like a 401k, 403b, or IRA) in order to grow in value and provide a financial asset that can generate future retirement income.

More madness of the payroll tax includes the annual Cost-of-living-adjustment (COLA), first introduced and reflected in benefits in 1975, following the 1973 SSA amendment. The purpose of these

OLAs is to annually adjust up the monetary value of SSA benefit
hecks to inflation, based upon change in the Consumer Price Index
CPI). While inflation has been very low the last eight years during
ne Federal Reserve's *quantitative easing* (QE) policy to keep interest
ates artificially low, any return to an average 2-to-3 percent inflation
rould mean Social Security benefits paid would almost double every
0 years, even as more and more new retirees join the benefit ranks.
ccording to the 2011 *Social Security Trustees Report,* this federal
ntitlement program is "not sustainable under its currently scheduled
nancing" and now runs a regular annual deficit. In 2011, and each year
nce (for the first time since 1983), Social Security failed to bring in
iore revenue than it spent. Even worse, this spending has exploded in
ie last four decades and is projected to increase at an even faster rate in
ie next four years. Several independent analyses and the SSA show the
rogram becomes insolvent in 2035 – it will not be able to pay benefits
it from those paying in. The next chapter looks at capital gains taxes.

---

esearch and analysis sources include: *TaxFoundation.org;
olitiact.com; ADP.com/ WageAndTaxFacts; Office of Management and
udget; PBS.org; The Congressional Budget Office; Federal-Tax-
ates.InsideGov.com; Bradford Tax Institute; U.S. Library of Congress
OC.gov); SSA.gov - Social Security Administration; IRS.gov;
heAtlantic.com; Medicare.gov; Forbes.com; TheAtlantic.com*

Chapter 15

Capital Gains Taxes

If You Invest Well, Be Ready To Share

"The politicians say 'we can't afford a tax cut' –
maybe we can't afford the politicians."

- Steve Forbes
Editor-In-Chief *Forbes*

Origin. The state sales tax is an indiscriminant *ad valore:* tariff or excise tax, and was frequently proposed throughou America's misguided history of taxation as the most logica alternative to the unapportionment of individually discriminatir among citizens with a *direct* tax on incomes. But after the 191 federal income tax was made a permanent part of the U.! Constitution, an entirely new set of questions started to be raise about *what* can be included in the definition of "income" by both th state and the federal governments. The debate eventually settled o the notion that the federal government can garner additional revenu off of private sector activities with a tax imposed on gains in valu

132

ver time on capital investments. These would include positive returns on stocks, bonds, mutual funds, precious metals, real estate, elling a business, and other invested funds. But the backlash from individuals and businesses that such taxation would dramatically reduce incentives for taking investment risks, prompted lawmakers to introduce the idea of re-classifying returns on asset values over me to be treated as unique from ordinary income like wages and alaries. Such a return would now be called a "capital gain" and be reported separately from ordinary income, and taxed at its own rate.

Rationale. The major problem with the original thinking that ains in asset values be treated (taxed) the same as ordinary income, as that it disregarded the basic concept that individuals and usinesses make capital investments with their *after-tax* incomes. hose funds have already been taxed, in many instances at both the deral and state level. If the owner of these after-tax funds then ants to buy stocks, bonds, or real estate, that investment carries herent risks about future performance – the values can go either p or down based upon a wide range of market factors. An *ordinary come* tax on any gains in value would add yet another layer of risk to the investment decision. To counter this type of misguided easoning, most conservative thinkers argued that capital gains are OT actually earned income, but are in fact changes in asset values er time, and are part of the fundamental capital investment activity the American private enterprise system, and must be treated fferently than regular, periodic cash-flow earnings.

The strongest argument for treating these differently is base on a key foundational accounting perspective. Individual salarie hourly wages, and business earnings from daily sales and operatir costs are by definition *Income Statement* transactions. On the othe hand, asset-value capital gains over time are by definition *Balanc Sheet* transactions. The former constitutes a regular, recurrir stream of income, while the latter is a one-time non-recurrir transaction related to a specific asset's value on a given day. Capit gains are then increases in the market value of established *after-tc* wealth that was originally purchased with *after-tax* "earning previously taxed by federal and even state governments.

The political compromise settled for taxing gains on asse held less than one year as *ordinary earned income* (like salaries ar wages, or pre-tax operating business income). Assets held at lea one year are then taxed at the preferential capital gains rate. Sad say, the holding period was now the deciding factor, not the inhere1 definition of the transaction. Either way, taxing capital gains is c *facto* double-taxation on both the private sector's *after-tax* earnc income (used to make capital asset investments), as well as on a1 positive gains in those asset values – the investment return on *afte tax* accumulated wealth. California is the only state that continur to tax all capital gains on asset values as *ordinary income*.

Table 15.1 summarizes the misguided history of capital gair tax rates in the U.S. For the most recent year of complete data, tl maximum rate was 15.35 percent on a relatively low $263 billion ains (2009 was just after the 2008 recession that officially ended in ane of 2009). The 2015 maximum rate reflects President Obama's isguided policy that raised the capital gains tax rate to 20 percent, hile adding a 3.8 percent surtax to help cover costs for Obamacare.

Table 15.1

6 DECADES OF U.S. CAPITAL GAINS TAXES
Maximum Rates + Effective Rates Paid

	Maximum Rate	Total U.S. Gains	Taxes Paid	Effective Rate
1954	25.0%	$ 7.15 Billion	$1.01 B	14.1%
1959	25.0%	$ 13.14 B	$1.92 B	14.6%
1964	25.0%	$ 17.43 B	$2.48 B	14.2%
1969	27.5%	$ 31.44 B	$5.28 B	16.8%
1974	36.5%	$ 30.22 B	$4.25 B	14.1%
1979	28.0%	$ 73.44 B	$ 11.75 B	16.0%
1984	20.0%	$140.51 B	$ 21.45 B	15.3%
1989	28.0%	$154.04 B	$ 35.26 B	22.9%
1994	29.2%	$152.73 B	$ 36.24 B	23.7%
1999	21.2%	$552.61 B	$111.82 B	20.2%
2004	16.05%	$499.15 B	$ 73.12 B	14.7%
2009	15.35%	$263.46 B	$ 36.67 B	13.9%
2015	23.80%	(not available) - - - - - - - - - - - - - - - -		

Sources: Tax Policy Center. Dept. of Treasury.
Office of Tax Analysis. The Motley Fool.

It's also worth noting that the peak capital gains reported in 199
included large stock market gains in that final year of that decade
dot.com-era (the market peaked in March 2000, then dropped ove
20 percent by year-end). The post-9/11 era of the Bush tax cuts als
had large capital gains reflected in the 2004 data.

The three benefits of capital gains taxes are: 1) preferential
lower rates than those paid on ordinary income (for 2015 the top ra
is 23.8 percent compared to the highest marginal income tax rate
39.6 percent); 2) tax deferral, meaning the tax is only due when tl
gain is "realized" (the asset is sold at the higher value), so that no ta
is due on any gain "on paper" that has not been realized; and 3) tl
stepped-up value basis allows investors to hold capital assets un
their death, at which time there is no capital gains tax due on tl
increased value over time, and the asset can be passed to others
the higher (stepped-up) value to begin a new cost basis.

Consider an example where an individual earns a salary ar
has paid federal taxes on that income. Those funds should now I
forever free from government intervention and completely at tl
discretion of the owner to decided what to do with them. With tl
after-tax funds under her discretion, she purchases 100 shares
common stock for $50 per share – a $5,000 capital investment (a
asset purchase). This decision is based on a plan to build weal
over time based on some acceptable level of risk. Five months late
she sells the stock at $65 per share for $6,500 and makes a $1,50
profit on her original $5,000 invested (a realized gain). But becau

he held the stock for less than a year, the IRS taxes that $1,500 profit as *ordinary income*, like her salary. This significantly reduces her realized net profit and also decreases her incentives for investing because making a return on an asset investment simply results in more (higher) "income" taxes levied. If it had been 15 months when the price hit $65 and she made that $1,500 profit, that would qualify or capital gains tax rates. Either way, she has already paid tax on those funds when she "earned" them, so the increase in wealth should now be hers to keep or reinvest at her discretion. But the IRS steps in and requires a tax. If she reinvests her original $5,000 plus her net after-tax capital gain, and that subsequently makes a $2,000 profit a year later, she has to again pay capital gains taxes.

The entire economic process of buying and selling that drives capital asset prices via supply and demand in the free market is based on the opportunity to make a profit on such investments based on the perceived risk assumed. *After-tax* income that is invested and reinvested multiple times during the course of a few years ends up being taxed several times. Noted billionaire Warren Buffet has proposed that capital gains taxes paid on assets should actually be *higher* – as in 30 percent of the realized profit. Imagine the negative impact a "Buffett-Rule" of 30 percent capital gains tax would have on the U.S. and global investment markets, by doubling the taxes due for: stock, bonds, mutual funds, precious metals, and real estate. He thinks that paying 30 percent capital gains tax on his investment return would be more in line with the 39.6 percent top tax rate on earned income. But not all asset investors are taxed in the top bracket. Taxing a long-term gain as if it was ordinary income increases the overall effective rates of double-taxation, while negatively impacting incentives for capital asset investments.

And of course, U.S. capital gains taxes are the sixth highest worldwide, with only Denmark (42 percent), France (34), Finland and Ireland (33), and Sweden (30) taking more from capital investment gains. The average of the 100+ countries in the Organization for Economic Cooperation and Development (OECD) is just 18 percent while nine nations have NO capital gains tax – and these tend to have the best GDP growth and job creation results. Can you imagine the huge volume of new capital investment that would occur in the U.S. if the capital gains rate was cut to say, 15 percent, or abolished altogether? That would certainly provide a major incentive for businesses to modernize infrastructure and invest in new hi-tech opportunities. The next chapter covers property taxes.

Research and analysis sources include: *TaxFoundation.org; Encyclopedia.com; Investopedia.com; Finance.Yahoo.com; Politiact.com; CharelsSchwab.com; Bradford Tax Institute; Forbes.com; IRS.gov; The Motley Fool; BankRate.com; TaxPolicyCenter.org; EconoLib.org*

Chapter 16

County Property Taxes

Every Year You Own It, You Pay

"The power of taxing people and their property is essential to the very existence of government."

- James Madison

Origin. The tax burden on individuals and businesses seemed if it could not become any more intrusive, right? Import-export riffs, excise taxes, federal income taxes, state sales taxes, state come taxes (even a city income tax in Gotham), payroll taxes, and pital gains taxes on investments together would appear to leave tle room for anything else to pay. And yet, the original debates out taxation among the founders included the prospects of an nual assessment on the total accumulated wealth of its citizens. is had strong historical precedent in the long history of feudal gland, as landowners paid a "per annum tribute" to the monarch, en as the serfs and tenants on the lords' lands paid an annual tax their smaller proportion of the overall estate. The goal of equality

within the colonies, and then the states, presented some diffict
ramifications for the American Congress, as landowners would
singled out for this additional tax, while renters would not be liab
This immediately created the impetus for tax strategies aimed
restructuring certain property holdings into third-party trusts
other forms of business, then the true owner could simply pay re
to the holding-trust and avoid the property tax.

After much discussion, that idea to tax total wealth each ye
lost support because of the incentive it would provide Americans
hide, or at least under-report, their cash, bank accounts, properti
and other assets, to avoid paying a portion of it to the feder
government each and every year. There were also concerns th
those with significant property and business holdings might not ha
the necessary cash flow liquidity each year to cover the combin
wealth tax, and would then be forced to sell tangible assets in ord
to raise funds to pay the tax. This would then create somewh
'forced sales' of asset holdings, and this idea was looked down up
by individuals, business owners, and politicians alike. The real est
(property) tax compromise had to then decide whether the tax wot
be incurred on buildings and other structures along with the land,
just the land, or on the structures and not the land. Lawmake
ultimately agreed that the value of the structures (but not the lar
was the most appropriate way to implement the property tax, whi
was widely justified as "such a small percentage of the value ea
year". But the reality is that over time (I have lived in my house 1

most 26 years) it can really add up – to as much as one third or ore of the property's total market value skimmed off and paid to the vernment over the course of 20, 30, or 40 years.

Today, individuals and businesses in the private sector pay operty taxes to their respective counties on the value of their mes, retail stores, apartments, warehouses, manufacturing sites, ice buildings – but not the land. The tax rates are typically tween one percent and two percent each year. The taxes collected en pay for local public services such as fire and ambulance, police d public safety, schools, salaries and wages for public employees, nitation, parks and recreation, libraries, cemeteries, roads, bridges, d other transportation infrastructure. For example, a 1.15 percent operty tax rate by itself in one year may not seem burdensome – er all, the owner is simply paying out a relatively small portion of e value to provide for essential local county services. A home with assessed value of $300,000 would then owe a property tax of ,450 – typically payable in two installments (April and December). it two things have been happening to property taxes in the U.S. th a very provocative impact on total payments over time.

First, virtually every local municipality has allowed property x rates to slowly increase over time. (Imagine government doing at?) It might have started at 1.15 percent for the initial few years, t then the law is amended or a new bond issue is approved by the ters and the rate slides up to 1.18 percent. At first glance that esn't seem like a big deal (that's only three 100ths of one percent, right? – just $90 added to the original $3,450 tax bill), but over the course of 20 or 30 years there could be a dozen or more of these seemingly "tiny" rate increases – each one seemingly insignificant in the year enacted; however, after three decades of ownership, the rate could hit 2.3875 percent, meaning, if the house remains taxed at its original $300,000 basis the annual property tax has gone up from $3,450 to $7,162 – more than double the original amount.

Rationale. The logic put forth by elected officials is that this is not that big of a deal, because the costs of all local municipal services that homeowners enjoy continue to go up over the course of those 30 years – to cover inflation adjustments, as well as expanded services and programs now offered by the local county government. It is also assumed that the homeowner's income has grown over that same time period so that the higher dollar value of property taxes paid is in all likelihood either a comparable portion of one's annual salary, or might even be a lower proportion if wages have gone up a a faster rate than the property tax increases over time.

As such, this opens up an interesting crossroads about the two different ways that property taxes are levied on households and businesses. Some municipalities re-assess every year all the home and commercial buildings within their jurisdiction. This means that the $300,000 home could next year be valued at $325,000 due to a strong local economy, so the same 1.15 percent tax rate increases the property tax due from $3,450 to $3,738. That almost $300 increase is then borne by the property owner because the home alue went up. Other states have enacted laws, like Proposition-13 ere in California, to keep property tax values fixed at the purchase rice, so while the tax rate may increase, it is always applied to the riginal purchase price. The only time a house or commercial uilding is re-assessed to a higher market value is when the property ; sold, establishing a stepped-up cost basis for the new owner.

Think of the various combinations of how property taxes can ıen impact homeowners and businesses in the private sector. The 'orst case involves having the property go up in value every year 'hile the property tax rate also increases over time. From the prior xample, that $300,000 home at 1.15 percent could in ten years be ssessed at $450,000 with a new rate of 1.785 percent. The property ıxes would go from $3,450 increase to just over $8,000 – more than oubling, because the economy is doing well AND the new legislated ervices, bonds, and other budget increases have been passed along) the property owners in the county to pay for. If the tax rate oesn't change over time (stays at 1.15 percent), and annual ssessed values are dropping (house now at $250,000), the property ıx would also drop to $2,875 from the original $3,450.

Madness. Even if the cost basis was held constant at the riginal price of $300,000 when purchased, the sliding scale of tax ıtes over time to 1.785 percent would still increase the property tax ıe to $5,355 – over $2,000 extra per year. Some municipalities ıat re-assess property values each year, have seen home prices and ısiness buildings stay flat for several years during a flat economy, or even drop in market value when the economy is in a recession.

they keep the tax rate constant when property values are constan

then their municipal government revenue stays flat, and the

impacts the budgets for schools, fire, police, parks, roads, the librar

– and that flat revenue always turns into a political issue for electe

officials and voters to debate regarding whether to increase the ta

rates to maintain government services. The big problem comes whe

property tax rates are raised to cover budget shortfalls, the econom

turns around and gets strong again, home and commercial buildin

prices rebound to higher values, only to be taxed at the new high

rate imposed when the economy and budget weren't doing so well.

Table 16.1 summarizes the ten states with the highest rates

property taxes in the nation. Notice that while New Jersey has th

highest rate and the highest median home price among these te

states, the much lower home prices in Nebraska and Texas still pu

these states on the top-10 list with rates at almost 2 percent. Th

gets right to the issue of placing the county's revenue burden o

private homeowners, even when home values are not anywhere nea

the highest in the nation. For example, my dollar value propert

taxes in Santa Barbara County, California (thanks to Proposition-1

are lower than seven of these ten, even though my home's mark

value is almost three times higher than the New Jersey media

priced home – the highest on this top-10 list. With average nation

property taxes at $2,089 (27 states adding another $423 average du

in vehicle property taxes) it's no surprise that the *National Tax Lie*

144

ssociation reports an estimated $11.8 billion of property taxes goes
npaid by homeowners and businesses every year nationwide.

Table 16.1

Highest Property Taxes in the U.S.
August - 2015

STATE	RATE	MEDIAN TAX PAID	MEDIAN HOME PRICE
New Jersey	2.38%	$7,331	$308,000
Illinois	2.32%	$3,939	$170,000
New Hampshire	2.15%	$5,017	$233,000
Connecticut	1.98%	$5,280	$267,000
Wisconsin	1.96%	$3,202	$163,000
Texas	1.90%	$2,510	$132,000
Nebraska	1.80%	$2,438	$133,000
Michigan	1.78%	$2,090	$118,000
Vermont	1.71%	$3,727	$218,000
Rhode Island	1.67%	$3,872	$232,000

Source: FiscalTimes.com

Table 16.2 lists the states that have the lowest property taxes
 the U.S. Notice that Hawai'i is at the very bottom because it
akes up for lower property tax revenues with its tourism industry,
llecting hotel surtaxes and other taxes on travel-related expenses.
any states rely on businesses to cover the majority of property tax

Table 16.2

Ten Lowest Property Taxes
For 2015 in the U.S.

STATE	AVERAGE TAX PAID	AVERAGE DMV TAX
Hawai'i	$ 482	- none -
Alabama	$ 752	$170
Louisiana	$ 832	- none -
Delaware	$ 917	- none -
South Carolina	$ 984	$416
D.C.	$1,001	- none -
West Virginia	$1,015	$378
Arkansas	$1,068	$239
Wyoming	$1,069	$413
Colorado	$1,089	$410

Source: WalletHub.com; U.S. Census Bureau;
State DMV vehicle files;

revenues, to reduce the burden on individual homeowners. The stat
of Wyoming has relatively low property taxes because almost 7
percent of property taxes are paid by firms involved in some form
mineral production. Nevada, right in the middle of the rankings a
number-24, brings in additional state revenues with casino taxes, a
well as hotel taxes similar to the tourism industry in Hawai'i.

Why do certain states and municipalities have much high
property taxes? The primary factor is often that the communit
might have really good schools, or at least very well-funded one
For example, the median residential property tax bill in New York

estigious Westchester County is $13,842 – highest in the country. feature article in *Westchester Magazine* focused on why the leafy, anquil county 30 minutes north of Manhattan has this dubious stinction. The report draws a comparison to Virginia's Fairfax unty, which tends to be similar in many ways to Westchester, as ey're both suburbs of big cities (New York and Washington, D.C.), ey have similarly high home values, and educate about the same umber of students in public schools (these have great reputations, d attract top quality teachers). However, Westchester spends over billion more to fund its schools, and since property taxes cover ost of that bill, there's a huge disparity in what homeowners tually pay. The average residential property tax bill in Fairfax is out $5,500 – just 40 percent of what Westchester residents pay. such, the average public school teacher salary in Fairfax was 7,000 in 2013-2014, while in Westchester it was $88,000. Benefits d administrative costs also add up, as Fairfax County has one hool superintendent while Westchester employs 40. The article ites: "Defenders of higher educator salaries always note that ey're necessary given the high cost of living in the area, and that is valid point, because even the teachers, principals, and perintendents *must also pay local property taxes*".

But many lawmakers understand that it's not simply spending ore money in ever-increasing budgets that translates into better ality public education. Wisconsin Governor Scott Walker clearly

recognized that, "In education, they say either property taxes have
go up, or we'll have poor education – that's a false choice".

New Jersey homeowners have arguably the country's highe
property taxes. The average bill in 2014 was $8,161. In fact, o1
study found that less than one percent of all homeowners in Ameri
pay more than $8,000 annually in property taxes. This Op-Ed fro
the *Asbury Park Press* noted the big reason for New Jersey's hig
property taxes is how much the state pays its government worker
The problem is not too many layers of government or excessi
numbers of state workers providing services, but the overly generou
salaries and benefits that public workers are paid. The average sta
worker salary is the highest in the nation, average teacher salary
third highest, and public employee health benefit costs are second
the U.S. In addition, 48 percent of state and local revenues collect
in New Jersey come from property taxes. This is ridiculously hig
because "No other state derives more than 41 percent of its reven
from that source, and the U.S. average is only 33 percent".

Of course, when a state or county has a high concentration
expensive homes, the average property taxes in that area will I
much higher. For example, Marin County in California (just north
San Francisco, right on the Pacific Ocean) has the most expensi
homes in the state, and with that, the highest property taxes as we
And yet, a *relative* property tax (based upon percentage of hon
value) shows that while $2 million to $5 million homes have t
highest relative rates, the second highest comes from poor

communities paying a baseline fixed dollar amount on homes valued under $50,000 – where their bill in dollars is not very large, but relative to the home value it's quite high. For example, a trailer park might charge a flat fee of just $750 a year for property taxes, but that's 2.25 percent if a double-wide is valued at $33,000. In the end it all comes down to having the correct assessed value on the home or commercial facility. The *National Taxpayers Union* estimates that between 30 percent and 60 percent of all properties are over-valued by their county assessor's office. Oh really? So while one can't change the legislated tax rate, it is possible to appeal and have the assessed value reduced, which then lowers the property tax due.

The next chapter examines perhaps the most odious tax in America – the inheritance tax (sarcastically known as the death tax), and the associated gift tax, that regulates how you decide to give away income and assets before you die.

Research and analysis sources include: *TaxFoundation.org; Money.com; Zillo.com; Westchester Magazine; Encyclopedia.com; Federal-Tax-Rates.InsideGov.com; Investopedia.com; Bradford Tax Institute; National Taxpayers Union; IRS.gov; The U.S. Constitution; EconoWed.UMD.edu; LincolnInst.edu; TaxWorld.org*

Chapter 17

Gift and Inheritance (Death) Taxes

You Thought By Dying You'd Be Done?

*"The difference between death and taxes is
death doesn't get worse every time Congress meets."*

- Will Rogers
American Humorist

Origin. By far one of the most bizarre taxation plans devised by federal lawmakers and presidential candidates has been targeting individual asset wealth for an inheritance tax *after* the person dies. This type of estate taxation (referred to as a "legacy" or "succession" tax) dates back to ancient Egypt, first-century Rome, and England's feudal era. Today's version began with the 1797 Stamp Act requiring all last wills and testaments to have an official government stamp in the probate court. During the 75 years up to the Civil War, Congress enacted an inheritance tax when funds were needed to finance various wars, and would repeal the tax when hostilities ceased. Remember, the first income tax was imposed with the 1861 Act, then implemented in 1862, to provide funding for the Union's war with th southern states. That law also included a new round of inheritance taxes, then a succession tax in the 1864 tariff law, but then the death tax was repealed in 1870. Four years later the law was challenged at the Supreme Court on the basis it was a *direct* tax, but the justices disagreed, and the tax remained in place.

Remember also the *Wilson-Gorman* law of 1894. It included estate-inheritance taxes, as well as a special provision for a "gift tax". The Supreme Court ruled against these on the basis they were in fact *direct* taxes. And for the next 20 years, there was no death tax, up until the 16th Amendment of 1913, which ushered in inheritance tax rates of one percent after a $50,000 exemption (about $10 million in today's terms), increasing steadily up to ten percent after $5 million. The rate was raised to 20 percent to help pay for WWI, but was not reduced when the war ended. Congress then added a gift tax in 1924 to thwart individuals from giving assets to each other as a way of avoiding the inheritance tax later after they died. Rates continued upward to 40 percent in the late 1920s, then 60 percent in the early 1930s, and hit a ridiculous 77 percent by the late 1930s into WWII – and stayed there into the mid-1970s, until the estate and gift taxes were unified into one system of tax rates and exemption credits. It dropped back to 55 percent in the 1980s and 1990s, when the exemption credits were increased. The Economic Growth Tax Act of 2001 (in response to the 9/11 terrorist attacks) put in place a phase-out of the inheritance tax by 2010, incrementally dropping the top rate while also raising the estate value exemption each year. But the

Obama Administration allowed that component of the Bush tax cuts to expire in 2011, and the law reverted to the 1997 levels with a top rate of 55 percent and a $1 million exemption.

In much the same way that capital gains taxes penalize a person twice (once for earning income, and then subsequently for making profits on asset investments made with *after-tax* assets), the federal government decided to perch the IRS (yes, just like a vulture eying the carrion) right on the sidelines when an individual dies to impose an *estate* tax on personal wealth.   This has sarcastically become known as the *death tax*.   Let's consider the lunacy of the logic behind such an invasion into one's personal life, even *after* death.   These assets were accumulated during a lifetime of paying taxes every year on earned income, plus double-taxation through capital gains taxes paid on profitable asset investments that went up in value, plus more double-taxation on cash dividends received from capital investments in stock.   So after 30, 40, 50 or even 60 years of paying all those taxes, when the individual dies and simply wants to leave all or portions of the estate to whomever he chooses, the federal government steps in once again and claims another round of taxes this time on the sum total of one's *after-tax* asset values.

Table 17.1 summarizes the misguided history of the death tax. Since the Estate Tax was first legislated in 1864, the   subsequent 1898 Legacy Tax, and the current Estate Tax (enacted in 1916) there have been twenty major revisions through 2001, and numerous on-again-off-again tweaks of the tax as recently as the 2010 year.

ng exemption from the death tax. The federal government justifies his personal confiscation of an individual's wealth on an archaic rationale that it helps avoid the over-concentration of wealth among

Table 17.1

150 YEARS OF ESTATE TAXES

1864	Between 1% and 6%
1898	Between ¾% and 15%
	Multiple definitions of siblings, uncles, charities, and other descendants.
1916	1% See: The Revenue Act of 1916.
1920s	15%-25%
1930s	25%-45%-60%
1940s	70% *Can you believe it was 70%?*
1950s	77% *Can you believe it was 77%?*
1960s	77%
1970s	77%
1980s	70%-65%-60%
1990s	55%
2000	55%
2001	55%
2002	50%
2003	49%
2004	48%
2005	47%
2006	46%
2007-2009	45%
2010-2012	35% *Included one-year hiatus in 2010.*
2013	55%

Source: U.S. Treasury

among a few powerful (legacy) American families. But the empirical reality is that such policy greatly discourages capital accumulation and cripples economic growth. It is inconceivable that the federal government could come in and siphon off 60 percent, 65 percent, 70 percent, and even as much as that top-rate 77 percent of an estate assets that were built over time (with various degrees of investment risk) using funds already previously taxed by the IRS. Granted there are certain exemptions that can limit this tax, based upon the value of the estate and to whom it is bequeathed, but that turns into a game of manipulated tax strategies to deal with this problem. The most important issue is the death tax should not be in place to start with, as it constitutes a gross invasion of privacy on personal assets already been taxed multiple times, and an individual's wealth should never be a tax revenue source targeted by the federal government.

As if the federal government's estate tax was not enough encroachment into the privacy of personal assets distributed after a person dies, the IRS also imposes a federal gift tax on a person's private decision to give cash or other assets to another person while still alive. As such, the government can reach in and confiscate a share of an individual's wealth, both while a person is alive and give to another (the gift tax), and then again after a person dies and give to another (the estate tax). There are also exemptions and income levels that must be navigated in the gift tax code to legally formulate a gift tax strategy (much like with death taxes), but the fundamental underlying issue remains: government should not be involved in ıxing legal transfers of *after-tax* cash and other assets between any vo parties in the private sector. The very fact that the IRS has a ook dedicated to understanding the rates and formulas for reporting nd calculating gift taxes and death taxes speaks volumes about the verbearing burden being imposed on its citizens with such a specific ıx. The gift tax was enacted in 1924, repealed in 1926 (it was eemed an over-reach of government's taxing power into the wealth f individuals), then re-enacted in 1932 under the rationale that it 'ould help minimize death tax avoidance by taxing those who tried) give away their estates prior to death. So essentially, the federal *ift tax* is in place to support the taxing power and code provisions of 1e federal *estate tax*. The 1916 tax act defined the modern era of state and gift taxes through 1975. Then in 1976, the federal code 'as updated to allow for the *generation-skipping* tax (pass an estate ıx-free now, but when that person dies the tax hammer falls), but 1is was phased out and then repealed in order to "... protect the 1tegrity of the [U.S.] income tax" (see: Luckey, *A History of Federal state, Gift, and Generation-Skipping Taxes,* 2003). The next chapter xamines four lesser-known, but very awkward tax matters.

---

esearch and analysis sources include: *TaxFoundation.org; ncyclopedia.com; Forbes.com; U.S. Master Estate And Gift tax Guide ?014); IRS.gov; IRS Code: Income, Estate, Gift, Employment, And xcise Taxes (2015); Estate And Gift Taxation 2nd Edition (2013).*

Chapter 18

AMT, Retirement Taxes, and Double Taxation

Who Comes Up With This Stuff?

"The problem is not that people are taxed too little, the problem is that government spends too much."

- Ronald Reagan

There are four other tax policies in the IRS code that must b examined, epitomizing more of the madness that is commonplace i America's misguided history: 1- the Alternative Minimum Tax (AMT 2- Social Security retirement income taxes, 3- Required Minimur Distributions taxes, and 4) Double Taxation. In each case, there i very little logic to how and why many of these taxes are assessed.

Origin. The AMT was devised in 1969 because individua corporate, trust, and estate tax filers were legally following the IR tax code to take write-offs, deductions, and exemptions that woul legitimately lower their final tax bill, but then politicians and the IR determined that those with "too high" of income levels should *not* b llowed to take advantage of these legal opportunities within the code, o that all of those adjustments are disallowed, and the resulting igher taxable income is then taxed at a higher rate. For example, chedule-A itemized deductions for state and local taxes, charitable iving, and mortgage interest, as well as the personal exemption for ependents are disallowed within the AMT. So once the tax-filer pends all the time, energy, and costs preparing the tax return, they ow have to pass a final test of their income level, to see if it is okay) use the legal code reductions to taxable income (that lowers their ixes due). If they don't meet the arbitrary income requirements set y the government, then the completed tax filing is deemed null and oid, and has to be recalculated with the "alternative" and "minimum" tipulations on a separate IRS Form-6251. The AMT requires taxes e done twice. The Tax Policy Institute famously dubbed the AMT he epitome of pointless complexity", and I firmly agree.

Congress and the IRS – in their infinite wisdom – picked a pecific level of personal, corporate, trust, or estate income as the rbitrary dividing line between "wealthy" and "not wealthy", to allow r not allow certain reductions to taxable income, which then kicks ι the AMT requirement. Even the IRS instructions state that having rst completed the regular tax forms, then doing them a second time ith the AMT rules, the taxpayer shall compare the two methods and s responsible for the higher of the two" (what else would we expect?). ι addition, the AMT cut-off point for income is not indexed for inflation, so as income increases each year, the hurdle for having to do the AMT remains the same. A very nice reward for getting a raise.

The second illogical tax involves one's Social Security income during the retirement years. Like me, many of you have received in the mail a form that shows all the years and income earned annually during which we paid into FICA. I smile (something very rarely done in the context of a government bureaucracy) when I see my Social Security earnings history start in 1982 with my first job at a Boston investment bank after I finished my MBA in finance. I also peruse the 28 years I was a university professor, and it's always a walk down memory lane to think about how much I made each year, when my four kids were born, when we bought our house. And at the end it shows the "estimated monthly income" I can expect if I start my checks at age 65 or age 67. But that's when the warm smiling stops. Having paid into the FICA system for perhaps 40 or 45 years, a person hits age 65 or 67 and decides to start collecting a monthly check from the SSA. Let the wonderful retirement years begin. But wait, the IRS views the monthly Social Security check as income, and requires individuals to declare it on Form-1040 and pay taxes on it.

The related third IRS tax happens with the Required Minimum Distribution (RMD) for retirement from private retirement plans like a 401(k), 403(b), 457(b), Simplified Employee Pension (SEP), traditional IRA, SEP-IRA, or profit-sharing plan at your company. If you have not started to take withdrawals on a monthly or quarterly basis by the time you reach age 70-and-a-half, then the IRS "requires" you to egin taking income from your funds, and of course, you have to pay ncome taxes on those distributions. (This won't apply to a Roth-IRA hat has different tax treatments on contributions and gains in value ver time.) This IRS requirement applies even if you don't yet need he money (you're still working full-time or part-time, or you own a usiness). And one other thought. You save for years to build up etirement assets of stocks, bonds, mutual funds, gold, and other nvestments, but using that for living expenses is simply *you* paying *ourself* from *your own* assets, and the IRS calls that taxable income. ut it's *your* money! You should be able to do with it what you like.

The RMD is calculated using the fund's account balance at the nd of the prior calendar year, divided by a distribution period factor om the misguided IRS "Uniform Lifetime Table" (it's encouraging to now that from their perspective, we all have a uniform lifetime head of us). But of course there is a separate table if the sole eneficiary is the fund-owner's spouse who is ten or more years ounger than the owner. That makes perfect sense, right? Those rophy-wives and gold-diggers deserve their own table. The IRS ounds out the unnecessary complexity by providing all kinds of orksheets to calculate the required amount, tables to find the RMD uring the participant or IRA owner's life, and even a "Joint Life And ast Survivor Expectancy Table" (I knew we'd all need one of those).

The fourth tax matter is "double-taxation" – where economic ctivity previously taxed by one statute, is then taxed again under a ifferent legal requirement. Three of the common examples include:

159

1) Someone has already paid income taxes on earnings and then decides to invest some of the *after-tax* funds into stocks, bonds mutual funds, or real estate. But when the investment has grown in value and is sold, that profit is taxed as a capital gain – even though the funds used for the investment were already previously taxed.

2) Shareholders in a company are paid a dividend, which must be reported as *ordinary income* on one's personal tax filing. But that dividend was paid with after-tax profits already taxed at the corporate rate. The federal government first taxes the corporation but then when the business wants to distribute some of the *after-tax* profits to its owners, a second tax is due to the IRS by each individual shareholder on that very same income.

3) An individual spends a lifetime paying taxes on wages, assets salaries, property, investments – and with the *after-tax* income each year saves, starts a business, invests in stocks, buys real estate - and on every transaction over the years pays taxes on interest earned dividends received, as well as any capital gains made as investments gained in value. When this person wants to gift some of these assets or after they die and simply want to leave the estate to family and friends (remember, these assets have been previously taxed multiple times over the years), the federal government steps in to take as much as 37 percent of those assets' value in both gift taxes and estate (death) taxes. These are both gross overreaches of government

The common factor (madness) among these four tax matters is the seemingly arbitrary cut-off points that lawmakers have decided

)on for things like: the earnings allowed before the AMT kicks in; at hat age to start Social Security benefits – 65 or 67, or wait a few ars for the law to change to 69 or maybe 70; the rationale for age)-and-a-half being the time that RMD must start; or that ten years the appropriate age-gap for having to do use an alternative table to lculate one's uniform life expectancy, taxing income in one manner ıd then taxing all or portions of that again in another context, and ıally, stepping in to tax gifts or estate bequests when all those sets are already *after-tax* values. We may chuckle and roll our eyes considering such minutiae in the IRS tax code, but the reality is is is how the tax system was written, and how taxpayers have to al with it. The next chapter looks at the penalties (excise tax) sociated with the Obamacare individual mandate.

---

search and analysis sources include: *TaxFoundation.org; ıcyclopedia.com; BankRate.com; TheFiscalTimes.com; Federal-Tax- ıtes.InsideGov.com; Forbes.com; Bradford Tax Institute; Tax Policy stitute; IRS.gov; H.S. Peckron - Alternative Minimum Tax: What You ed To Know About The 'Other' Tax (2004); The Problem Of Double xation (Economica, June 1926); Schwab.com*

Chapter 19

Obamacare Penalty Taxes

Something New For The I.R.S. To Do

"Did you ever notice that when you put the words
'THE' and "IRS' together it spells 'Theirs' ?"

- Henny Youngman
American Comedian

Origin. When Barack Hussein Obama became president i
2009, he had a Democrat majority in both the House and Senat
These allowed him to introduce the *Patient Protection and Affordab*
Care Act (Obamacare) on September 17, 2009 (barely seven month
after he took office) with little overall resistance to a fairly clear pat
to becoming law. The House barely approved the bill 219-212, an
then the Senate voted 60-39 to approve, and it was signed into la
on March 23, 2010. There was such a rush to get the bill passed an
avoid any meaningful discussion in Congress not a single Republica
voted for the bill. We all remember the infamous statement fro
then-House speaker Nancy Pelosi, "It's going to be very, very excitin,
[but] we first have to pass the bill so you can find out what's in i

vay from the fog of the controversy". Well, it took several months to ally find out exactly what this new law would mean on multiple onts – who would be covered, how would that happen, what would cost, and what would be covered?

Rationale. Perhaps the most dubious of the provisions was e "individual mandate" that started in January 2014 stating "most nericans [must] obtain and maintain health insurance, or an emption, each month or pay a tax penalty on your federal income x form, and this fee goes up each year from 2014-2016, so it's portant to look into coverage and exemption options". The key hite House rationale is that "Congress has the power to levy taxes its citizens", so the mandate "tax" would be okay. But the White use budget director Jeff Zients stated unequivocally that it was _not_ "tax", just a "penalty fee". Even the head of Health and Human rvices, Kathleen Sebelius, told a Congressional hearing that it perates the same way a tax would, but it is _not_ per se a tax". And President Obama's infamous September 2009 interview, George ephanopoulos read the *Merriam-Webster's Dictionary* definition of a x" and asked how the insurance mandate penalty could not be ything other than a tax. The president replied, "I don't care what e dictionary says, it's not a tax . . . this levy is for your own good".

Madness. The thinking behind this penalty tax is that people uld rather pay for insurance than pay the fine for not having verage – as Obama declared, government does this for our good. e madness continues in that everyone must first determine if they are in the penalty area or not, based upon whether the exemptio applies. For 2016, the exemption is defined as any of the following:

- income under $10,350 for singles,
- income under $20,700 for married couples,
- $13,350 for heads of households,
- coverage cost exceeds 9.56 percent of your income,
- suffered a hardship in obtaining coverage,
- have only a short-term gap in being covered,
- opt out based upon religious grounds,
- not a U.S. citizen or national,
- incarceration (prison), or
- member of a recognized Native American tribe.

The real madness is the Obamacare website's pitch: "Why pay th penalty if you could get a subsidy instead?" Those subsidies going t over 80 percent of Obamacare sign-ups, are being paid for by highe insurance premiums charged to those who *can pay* for policies. Th penalty tax is very confusing to calculate. It is either, A) two percer (2015) of your income above the minimum level to file a tax retur (2.5 percent in 2016), or B) a $695 penalty times the number c uninsured persons in your household (not to exceed three times tha penalty, or $2,085). If under age 18, the penalty is cut in half. Alsc the penalty can't be larger than the national average for the lowes cost Obamacare policy. For example, the 2015 "bronze" coverag averaged $207 per month per person, or $1,305 for a family of five.

There were still 33 million uninsured people in the U.S. i

014 *after* Obamacare has been in place for five years. The IRS stimates that 12 million people qualify for the exemptions, while 7.5 illion people will have to pay the penalty tax. The IRS reported that r 2014, tax filers subject to the penalty paid on average $200 per erson, and this will go way up in 2016 and 2017. The penalty is a *rogressive tax* that increases proportionately (and substantially) lative to income. For example, a family with income of $500,000 oesn't sign up, so it owes a $12,000 penalty tax in 2016. The 2016 enalty for a middle-class family of four earning $60,000 is $2,085. his effective 3.5 percent tax is in addition to their federal income tax, nd any state income tax (where applicable).

The IRS added Form-8965 to report one's exemption status. aving minimum required coverage is reported by checking a new ox on Form-1040. Employers, healthcare providers, and the health xchange marketplace must now issue a new Form-1095 to everyone onfirming their coverage status, and this also gets reported to the S. This entire fiasco is nothing more than another layer of illogical ureaucratic complexity giving the IRS more ways to collect taxes. he next chapter looks at Obama's desire to tax internet use.

esearch and analysis sources include: *TaxFoundation.org; ncyclopedia.com; FoxNews.com; RealClearPolitics.com; Politiact.com; ongressional Globe Archives; PBS.org; Forbes.com; USNews.com; radford Tax Institute; ObamacareFacts.com, Healthcare.gov; IRS.gov; ealthInsurance.org; Kiplinger.com; MarketWatch.com*

Chapter 20

Obama Wants An Internet Tax

You're Kidding, Right?

> *"President Obama is leaning heavily on the*
> *Federal Communications Commission (FCC),*
> *an independent agency, to change the Internet*
> *from a competitive, free-market service*
> *into a government-regulated public utility."*

> \- Phil Kerpen
> AmericanCommitment.org

One major lesson everyone learned in 1980 when Microwave Communications, Inc. (MCI) won its lawsuit against America Telephone & Telegraph (AT&T), was that removing government fees pricing restrictions, and monopoly policies that reduce competition led to better phone quality, lower prices, and more incentives for private capital investment to improve technology infrastructure, as well as continuous innovation in both products and services. The gates were opened wide for nationwide and global competition in markets, phone products, choices in pricing plans, and strategic partnerships. Every individual and business benefitted in free market competition, and most importantly, operating costs for lecommunications started three and a half decades of continuous ductions due to ever-improving technologies and the huge volume new users that sprang up due to massive increased demand.

The global internet (worldwide web) launched and developed in e free-market environment of the 1990s. This was a second decade technology innovation infrastructure expansion for the telecomm dustry, and it spread well beyond lowering rates on phone calls, to clude cable television, online communications (email), cellular one service, and all kinds of wireless systems such as WiFi and oud storage and computing. With such an astounding track-record competitive success worldwide, it is inconceivable that President bama and a "government knows best" mindset (and accompanying ireaucratic advisors – the same kinds of misguided minds that ought us Obamacare and the 2009 federal "stimulus", have since)08 been lobbying for an usage-tax on the internet.

Origin. The terribly misguided perspective begins with Obama id Julius Genachowski – his hand-picked appointee to head the ederal Communications Commission (FCC) – eying the massive chnology infrastructure daily volume of Web traffic and applying at classic federal-lack-of-understanding that thinks, "If we charged st a few pennies on every transaction, no one would miss that, and would bring in potentially tens – or even hundreds – of billions of illars we could spend on all kinds of new government programs". 2012 the FCC proposed replacing the archaic Universal Service ind (taxes and surcharges on cellular and landlines still buried in your 10-page phone bill), that have grown from 5.5 percent in 199{ to 15.3 percent today) with the hip-sounding "Connect America Fun that is nothing more than a *broadband excise tax* on internet usage.

Rationale. The impetus for such a devastating tax goes bac to 2001, right on the heels of the 1990s dot.com era of massi\ internet expansion, when two complementary bills from Senat< Byron Dorgan (D-N.D.) and Ernest Istook (R-Okla.) had bipartisa support in the House and Senate to authorize the creation of a stat< run taxing cartel that would collect a *sales tax* on all cross-bord< commerce, including Internet-facilitated. Over half the states ha\ expressed interest in participating in such nationwide e-Sales ta: however, the U.S. Constitution is very clear that state governmen\ are generally prohibited from taxing or regulating any interstat commerce. But Congress can override the restriction and sanctio such an anti-competitive arrangement. This national "Net" sales ta idea laid the groundwork for Obama advocating a Web usage tax.

It's very hard to comprehend that Sprint and Google actual\ supported the initiative, because this federal program is supposed \ do some good, by developing technology to connect some 19 millio Americans who still don't have high-speed web access in their are< Remember, throughout this book, the common misguided feder< government theme remains: "taxes will correct a perceived injustice Genachowski argues that broadband web technology is vital for eve\ segment of the nation to be productive and competitive in the 21 century. But isn't the decision to expand coverage to that 19 millio

emographic one that should (and must) be made by private sector
ternet service providers (ISPs), based upon market opportunities
)out supply, demand, and expected return on capital investment?

Madness. Obama's plan would impose a new 16.1 percent tax
1 your Internet bill, and this automatically rises every three months
all without the approval of elected representatives in Congress.
roadband internet is the greatest infrastructure success story in
merica. While private investment has driven remarkable growth
1d innovation for the telecommunications Web, in contrast, our
ater, sewer, power, and transportation infrastructure – largely run
/ government with tax dollars – are, to put it kindly, not doing
:arly as well. What has an initial appearance of a new plan to do
)me good, will of course ultimately introduce price controls, service
efficiencies, and higher costs for all users. These will have a
)mpounding negative effect on how the web is accessed, by whom,
1d for how long, while setting up yet another layer of federal
1reaucracy to limit the free-flow of information for individuals and
1sinesses. How will the FCC implement such a tax? Will it be a flat
te on everyone's bill? Or perhaps a "pay-as-you-go" method with a
eter that ticks along whenever you're logged on. Imagine all the
ays companies (and individual programmers) will be incentivized to
1d alternative forms of access that will bypass paying the tax. I
1mediately think of how when I travel to China (where web access is
)vernment-controlled and limited), I use a virtual private network
PN) to bypass the PRC's censor of most websites. This allows me

to connect my Mac to a WiFi signal in my Beijing or Shanghai hot that routes my web-access through Miami, New Zealand, or Canad while the Chinese web-agents who are no doubt monitoring me, se only a blind connection to a generic uncensored site on their grid.

It is ridiculous to try and imagine the kind of bureaucrac monitoring, reporting, and enforcement that would have to b instituted to tax all types of access to the web. Who, besides ou president, looks at the state of all infrastructure in America and see the Internet as the problem area? There is an even more concret problem with Obama's plan, as it will replace private investment wit taxes that will hit every American individual and business.

Former FCC commissioner Harold Furchgott-Roth knew tha "classifying broadband access services as 'interstate telecomn services, those would suddenly become required to pay FCC fees; a 16.1 percent, it would be perhaps the largest, one-time tax increas on the Internet". It will only get worse from there, because the ta will go up every three months *without* a vote of Congress – and the is every reason to believe that private investment would declin forcing the new tax higher. On Wall Street, Obama's plan is know as the "nuclear option" because of the devastating effect it woul have on private capital investment. In fact, AT&T has put on ho billions of dollars in new fiber-optics networks to about 100 cities.

Has anyone stopped to ask what exactly the problem is tha we're trying to solve? Even Bill Clinton's favorite think tank, th *Progressive Policy Institute,* opposes the Obama internet tax warnin is "inconsistent with the Democratic Party's legacy". After all, the ternet took off in the early 1990s, thanks in significant degree to e 'light touch' approach on regulation of the Clinton Administration. hen was the last time anybody said: "The Internet has really gone wnhill since it was opened up to private commercial development"? ho looks at the bad old days of monopoly public utility regulation th Ma-Bell and says: "The Internet would be so much better if it rked liked the former telephone system"?

The push for the Obama plan comes from two constituencies: rent-seeking video giants like Google/YouTube, and NetFlix who ink a taxpayer-funded, government-regulated utility will guarantee em zero-cost access to customers, and 2) ideological extremists like bert McChesney who has said: "the ultimate goal is to get rid of e media capitalists in the phone and cable companies and to divest em from control". For anyone who isn't a huge web-content firm far-left liberal, federally taxing and regulating the Internet is a rrible idea. Instead, the key issue should not be finding more ivate sector activities to tax, but limiting the gross over-spending bits of all levels of federal, state, and local governments. The next apter reviews the last 40 years of attempted tax reform.

---

search and analysis sources include: *TaxFoundation.org; ashingtonTimes.com; TheNewAmerican.com; IRS.gov; Forbes.com; allStreetJournal.com; Cato.com; USNews.com; NationReview.com; gitalTrends.com; Google.com/TakeAction; Heritage.org; Time.com*

Chapter 21

Prior Attempts At
Tax Reform: 1976-2016

Note The Key Word, "Attempts"

*"This nation should have a tax system that
looks like someone designed it on purpose."*

- William E. Simon
former Treasury Secretary

The above quote, while funny in its delivery, provides a ve₁
succinct commentary on the misguided history of American taxe
The current IRS tax code reflects the uncoordinated piecemeal way
has been put together over the last 100 years. It is uncoordinated i
its logic, tedious in format, vague in its intent, irrational in its rule
and utterly confusing in the language of its countless procedur₁
explanations. To the import-export tariff was added a domestic exci₁
tax, to which was added the *direct* income tax, then taxes o
inheritances and gifts (to avoid the death tax), then payroll mandat₁
to social programs, taxes on gains in capital assets, and anoth₁
mandate to enroll in government healthcare or pay a penalty tax – a
on top of state income, sales, and property taxes. Every year the IR

lls out new forms, different schedules, updated tax tables, modified
emptions, and changes to certain provisions. But a broken system
oesn't really need *reform*: some adjustments within the existing
ructures. Instead, the tax code needs *replacement* – scrapping
hat has become so wasteful, confusing, and burdensome, and
utting in its place an efficient, logical, easy-to-use code that uses
mmon sense – *one that looks like someone designed it on purpose.*

Origin. For the last 40 years, there have been attempts at tax
form. There were a few minor tweaks to the code in the late 1970s
hen even the Treasury Department published its classic *Blueprints*
or *Basic Tax Reform* (1977, Foreword by the same William Simon
ho provided this chapter's opening quote). Arguably the two most
mportant attempts happened first in 1981, with Ronald Reagan's
conomic Recovery Tax Act (ERTA) that cut taxes across-the-board by
5 percent for individuals and businesses, and second, Reagan's
86 Tax Reform Act that cut the top individual tax rate from 50
ercent to 28 percent, and the corporate rate from 50 percent to 35
ercent. During the 1990s, President Clinton added earned income
edits that 'refunded' money to individuals who had not even paid
r owed) any tax in the first place. Then the Bush tax cuts in 2001
lped the economy avoid a much-anticipated recession after 9/11,
ut he also expanded tax credits and Medicare benefits.

And while there have been plenty of tax increases since 1976,
ore forms to fill out, higher tax rates to pay, new ways to siphon off
ivate sector income for government bureaucracy, and continued

frustration with time wasted on monthly, quarterly, and annu
compliance – most attempts at *reform* have been modest – lowering
few tax rates, or closing a few loopholes. There have been sever
notable voices calling out nationally with plans to completely *repla*
the broken tax code, even proposing the abolition of the IRS
implementing a radically simplified code and a common 1-page for
for both individuals and businesses, while also eliminating thin
like capital gains and inheritance/gift taxes altogether.

Rationale. Typical reforms begin with the premise of how
bring in the same total tax revenue, while eliminating most (or all)
the compliance burden.   It is the most basic logic that everyor
should readily agree with, that if all the forms, schedules, rules, ar
tables can be eliminated, with the same amount of tax collected, wh
would anyone oppose saving all that wasted time and money?   Bu
tax reform always finds opposition from those who benefit from th
current system.   One notable proposal came in 1992 when curre
California Governor Jerry Brown campaigned for the Democrat
presidential nomination, advocating a 13 percent flat tax for bo
individuals and corporations, designed for him by former Reaga
economic advisor Arthur Laffer.   Brown was ridiculed and labeled
dreamer by special interest groups (tax attorneys, tax accountant
certain trusts, and many corporations that use the existing code
reduce or avoid paying taxes each year).

During the Republican presidential primaries in 1996, Ste
Forbes made a very persuasive argument for a 17 percent flat ta

at he famously said could be filed on a form the size of a postcard. e 2012 Republican presidential primary included former *National staurant Association* CEO Herman Caine proposing his "9-9-9" flat x, while then-Texas Governor Rick Perry advocated his "20-20-20" t tax. Many 2016 Republican presidential candidates have offered t-tax ideas, including Ted Cruz (10 percent on individuals and 16 rcent on corporations), Ben Carson ("somewhere around 15 rcent"), Rand Paul (14.5 percent individual income tax and 14.5 rcent business "Value-Added Tax"), and Marco Rubio (25 percent individuals and corporations). Donald Trump wants zero taxes on lividuals making $25,000 (married couples making $50,000) – moving 75 million people from paying taxes, with four brackets for e rest of the nation (0, 10, 20, and 25 percent), a 15 percent rporate tax, and eliminating the AMT, marriage penalty, and leritance (death) tax. Jeb Bush proposes just three personal tax tes (28, 25, and 10 percent), eliminating most tax "loopholes", and 20 percent corporate rate. Chapter 25 discusses these ideas and ler common sense solutions like the "fair tax" that eliminates all :ome taxes, replacing them with a national consumption tax on all rchases of goods and services.

Meaningful tax reform has to fully embrace William Simon's ote – that it's time once-and-for-all to have a tax code that "looks e someone designed it on purpose". The key element of such a m would be removing all the wasted time and 70,000 pages of gulations, and completely replacing these with a simplified system that is revenue-neutral – bringing in the same total net tax dolla collected as the old system. In today's terms that means a radica new tax plan that can still generate just over $3 trillion annually.

Madness. We have all watched in disbelief over the last 10- years as the House and Senate bickered back and forth over a min update to the IRS tax tables, or slightly different versions of who ge a newly-proposed tax credit. We saw them argue about whether extend the Bush tax cuts or let them expire. They cheered f themselves as they temporarily reduced the payroll tax, to put mo take-home pay in people's checks (that reduction was of course ve temporary and ultimately reverted to the regular 15.3 percent rat The 2015 year-end had Congress again fighting over whether make permanent a huge list of special interest tax credits that cov public school-teacher classroom expenses, new racetracks develope by NASCAR owners, citrus and nut growers, the film industry, ar real estate investment trusts (REITs). In 2016, lawmakers are set consider taxes on craft beers and micro-breweries, even as the onli sales tax tries a comeback, alongside supposed bipartisan tax 'refor ideas for business taxation – as long as they include increases in tl earned income credit tax (EICT) for low income individuals.

The most frustrating facet of proposing radical tax change the intense resistance it gets from lobbyists committed to keeping tl existing code and structures in place. The two most powerful grou that continue to support current IRS laws are: A) tax professiona (accountants, attorneys, planners, advisors) whose skills won't l eded if a simple, common sense tax reporting and payment system adopted, and B) corporations and trusts in certain industries that rive huge tax breaks from the current code, allowing them to pay tle or no taxes by using legal write-offs and income reclassification ovisions. These two groups have nothing to gain from a common nse, easy tax code, so their Washington, D.C. lobbyists work hard influence politicians away from supporting any changes, while eping the same 70,000-page monstrosity in place.

Ultimately, it requires a political "outsider" who has no links th lobbyists and special interest groups – someone who can clearly ake the common sense argument to the American people so tax de replacement can gain popular support among all individual and isiness taxpayers. It simply requires strong leadership to look past e hurdles of a 100-year old entrenched system and provide a mpelling alternative that replaces all the waste and irrational gulatory language with an efficient and logical plan that is revenue-utral. The next chapter takes a look at the government largess that rpetuates the misguided history of American taxes.

---

search and analysis sources include: *TaxFoundation.org; Federal-rbes.com; Investopedia.com; LATimes.com; Time.com; USNews.com; nate.gov; TheAtlantic.com; IRS.gov; NYTimes.com; Fortune.com; ito.com; History.com; NPR.org; CPA2Biz.com; Investopedia.com; xHistory.org; Time.com; USNews.com; GovTrack.us; NYTimes.com*

Chapter 22

Federal Spending, Deficits, Debt, And Taxes

Government Always Wants More

"The problem is not that people are taxed too little, the problem is that government spends too much."

"We don't have a $3 trillion debt because we haven't taxed enough, [but] because we spend too much."

- Ronald Reagan

Origin. What do federal spending, deficits, the national debt and taxes have in common? They continued to go up every year with no end in sight. Once government gets a certain tax started, is virtually impossible for it to be cut back, let alone be rescinde Lawmakers get used to those tax revenues and have no ability control overspending that creates huge annual deficits, alway adding to massive Treasury debt. Their political lives are depende on those programs and tax funds already appropriated. As such, th House, Senate, President, state legislatures and governors, coun supervisors, even local city councils are always thinking of new wa o spend *our* money, so they have to devise new ways (taxes) to raise additional revenues from private sector individuals and businesses.

The prior chapters have taken you through a very misguided history that started with a revolution prompted in part by a major tax problem. There were import-export tariffs and a domestic excise tax – then reluctantly the income tax (1861, 1862, 1864) to support the Civil War. That was repealed (1872) seven years after the war ended. Twenty years later (1894) it is was tried again, then struck down by the Supreme Court. After another twenty years (1913), the income tax was amended to the Constitution. Twenty more years (1935) passed and Social Security required a payroll tax. Inheritance, gift, sales, capital gains, and property taxes, along with state (and even city) income taxes were added over time. Thirty years later (1965) added a mandatory entitlement (Medicare) to payroll taxes. This incredible tax burden is now entrenched in American life.

Rationale. *Government does not have its own money.* It only has funds it confiscates from citizens through taxes and fees, so it is completely dependent on collecting these. Cutting taxes, on the other hand, requires cutting spending (ouch), and developing self-restraint (ouch), and that means smaller budgets (ouch) with less workers on federal payrolls (ouch) at places like the Departments of Education, Commerce, Transportation, Energy, Health and Human Services, Housing and Urban Development, and Labor. Always remember the public sector does not generate new revenue, profits, create wealth, but instead draws funds (capital) directly away from the enterprising activities throughout the private sector by taxatic and fees to fund out-of-control public sector spending programs.

The widespread misconception is that government revenu come from productive activities, the same way enterprising actio by innovative entrepreneurs and firms in the private sector genera revenues from products and services they sell, and on which th make a profit. However, when people make statements such a *"Money coming from Washington will be allocated for this program"*, "More *government funds* are needed", the common thinking is th the federal government somehow has a huge pile of cash that ha mysteriously appeared in our nation's capital, and it belongs politicians to spend on programs they believe are important. To son degree government does have a cash pipeline – the power to ta individuals and businesses in the private sector, so what shou really be said is something like: *"Government will raise my taxes, ar take more of my money to pay for expanded social programs"*, becau that's what actually happens. Federal and state governments do n have stockpiles of cash generated from dedicated economic sources.

Milton Friedman noted: "Government gets the money it spenc [from] increased taxes, borrowing from the public, and creating ne money; getting extra taxes requires raising the rate of taxation, [an as a result, the taxpayer gets to keep less of each dollar earned as return on investment, which reduces [the] incentive to work and save, [so] the resulting reduction in effort or savings is a hidden co of the extra spending" (1978 Friedman lecture in Erie, PA). Fisc mmon sense seems to be a thing of the past, while overspending is w ingrained in all government activities – but it was not always the se. In his 1925 inaugural address, Calvin Coolidge said:

"I favor the policy of economy, not because I wish to save money, but because I wish to save people. The men and women of this country who toil are the ones who bear the cost of the Government. Every dollar that we carelessly waste means that their life will be so much the more meager. Every dollar that we save means that their life will be so much the more abundant. Economy is idealism in its most practical form".

overnment programs and taxes to pay for them may have started th good intentions, maybe even a feasible economic model to make em work – remember Social Security was launched with just a one rcent payroll tax and 159 workers paying in to support one person ceiving benefits. But over time, the original financial metrics are no nger sustainable or viable. The federal government spends the tax venue it collects on literally thousands of initiatives, programs, encies, and services – always under the rationale (ruse) of making e better, fixing a problem, or righting a wrong in society.

Madness. In each of the last seven years, Congress has never proved a federal budget on time (and so our annual saga about nether to shut down the government). In March of 2012 the House ted down Obama's 2013 budget 414-to-0 due to continued record-tting deficits over $1 trillion – just one year after his 2012 budget s brought to the Senate and the motion to introduce it was voted wn 97-to-0. In each case, ALL Democrats joined ALL Republicans

and no one sided with the president. When government spends mor
than it brings in, it creates deficits paid for by Treasury borrowing
Each year of deficits keeps adding to the total national debt – an
like your personal credit card, if you keep doing new charges ever
month, it adds to your outstanding balance. But unlike Visa c
Mastercard that limit how much credit is extended to you, there i
virtually no limit to how much the U.S. Treasury can borrow, so th
national debt just continues to grow every year. And so those craz
Congressional debates to (always) extend the nation's debt limit.

There have been three 2-term presidents from 1993 to toda:
The total debt incurred by the prior 41 presidents (1789-1992) wa
$4.3 trillion during 203 years. Table 22.1 shows federal spending
deficit or surplus, and total U.S. debt during the years of Presider
Clinton (1993-2000). His first year in office he increased spending b
two percent, then added $1.27 trillion in debt during his eight years

Table 22.1 - Clinton

	ANNUAL SPENDING	SURPLUS	(DEFICIT)	TOTAL DEBT
1993	$ 1.41 T		($ 255 B)	$ 4.35 T
1994	$ 1.46 T		($ 203 B)	$ 4.64 T
1995	$ 1.52 T		($ 164 B)	$ 4.92 T
1996	$ 1.56 T		($ 107 B)	$ 5.18 T
1997	$ 1.60 T		($ 22 B)	$ 5.37 T
1998	$ 1.65 T	+ $ 69 B		$ 5.48 T
1999	$ 1.70 T	+ $126 B		$ 5.61 T
2000	$ 1.79 T	+ $236 B		$ 5.62 T

Table 22.2 shows spending (deficit or surplus), and total debt for President Bush (2001-2008). His first year he increased spending by 3.9 percent, then added $4.22 trillion to the debt in his eight years.

Table 22.2 - Bush

	ANNUAL SPENDING	SURPLUS	(DEFICIT)	TOTAL DEBT
2001	$ 1.86 T[1]	+ $128 B		$ 5.76 T
2002	$ 2.01 T		($ 158 B)	$ 6.19 T
2003	$ 2.16 T		($ 378 B)	$ 6.76 T
2004	$ 2.29 T		($ 413 B)	$ 7.35 T
2005	$ 2.47 T		($ 318 B)	$ 7.91 T
2006	$ 2.65 T		($ 248 B)	$ 8.45 T
2007	$ 2.73 T		($ 161 B)	$ 8.95 T
2008	$ 2.98 T		($ 458 B)	$ 9.94 T

Table 22.3 then shows spending, deficits (no surpluses), and total debt for the recent seven years under President Obama (2009-2015). His first year he increased spending a huge *18 percent*, then added

Table 22.3 - Obama

	ANNUAL SPENDING	SURPLUS	(DEFICIT)	TOTAL DEBT
2009	$ 3.52 T		($1.413 T)	$11.88 T
2010	$ 3.47 T		($1.294 T)	$13.53 T
2011	$ 3.61 T		($1.299 T)	$14.76 T
2012	$ 3.54 T		($1.087 T)	$16.05 T
2013	$ 3.45 T		($ 680 B)	$16.72 T
2014	$ 3.51 T		($ 485 B)	$17.79 T
2015	$ 3.69 T		($ 440 B)	$18.12 T
2016	*$ 4.00 T*		*($ 474 B)*	*$19.35 T*

over $8 trillion to the national debt in just seven years. The Congressional Budget Office (CBO) projects that with fiscal year 2016 included (in italics), when Mr. Obama leaves office, he will have added $9.4 trillion to the national debt during his eight years – an average of almost $1.2 trillion per year. And be sure to notice how federal government spending has skyrocketed from $1.41 trillion in 1993 to right at $4 trillion in the current 2016 budget. That's nearly a 300 percent increase, so it's easy to see why politicians continue to resist tax cuts and any tax changes. They only know over-spending!

More Madness. In the six decades since WWII, all taxes have averaged around 19 percent of the total domestic economy (Hauser's Law) – almost one fifth of all U.S. economic activity. Federal spending on *mandatory* entitlements (Social Security, Medicare, Medicaid) is now 65 percent (two-thirds) of the annual budget. USDebtClock.org reports that total federal unfunded liabilities (all future obligations the government is responsible for) are now $127 trillion. This break down (literally) to over $1.1 million per taxpayer, and equals the total global GDP of 2012. The Washington Post (2013) reported the total net worth of America is $94 trillion – which means the U.S. has outstanding obligations that are $30 trillion higher than the total value of the nation's wealth. Government cannot continue to create and support social welfare programs for which it has no ability to pay.

Benjamin Franklin stated his position on government over-spending on social programs: "I am for doing good to the poor, but differ in opinion of the means. I think the best way is not making em easy in poverty, but leading or driving them out of it. I [have] served in different countries, that the more public provisions were made for the poor, the less they provided for themselves, and of course [they] became poorer. And, on the contrary, the less was done for them, the more they did for themselves, and became richer".

Benjamin Franklin
2nd Continental Congress
(1775 – 1778)

More and higher taxes have led to less economic growth and ss total tax revenues collected. Higher taxes have stifled economic owth and crippled job creation. Increased government spending ith less tax revenues collected has required outrageous federal rrowing to cover these deficits. In 2012, then-Treasury Secretary m Geithner reported to the House Budget Committee on President

Obama's 2013 proposed spending saying it would "stabilize" federa deficits over the next ten years. Did you hear that spin? That's very deceptive term, meaning the huge escalation in deficits would d nothing more than "stabilize" (remain at historically high levels) – bu won't have significant deficit reduction. When challenged by Pau Ryan, "So you have no plan to get debt under control", Mr. Geithne replied: "You are right, we're not coming with a definitive solution t that problem; what we do know is we don't like yours" (referring t Ryan's entitlement reform and deficit-reduction plan). So there yo have it. There is no plan to get federal deficit-spending under contro and only continued denial that the U.S. is heading toward a financia crisis threatening the core of the private sector economy, as deficit and debt continue to accumulate at record levels. Another 5-7 year of unchecked deficits will put the national debt at over 110 percent o GDP – the same level as Greece, Spain, Italy, and Portugal when the sparked the European debt crisis of 2013. The next chapter looks a how over-burdensome taxes limit our freedom.

Research and analysis sources include: *LATimes.com; IRS.go USGovernmentSpending.com; Washington Post; TaxFoundation.or FactCheck.org; USDebtClock.org; Congressional Research Service; U.S Office of Personnel Management; National Review; WSJ.co FoxNews.com; Forbes.com; CNN.com; EconoMonitor.com; NYTimes.co USGovernmentSpending.com*

Chapter 23

Taxes Limit Freedom

Everywhere We Go, Everything We Do

"In 1790, the nation which had fought a revolution against taxation without representation discovered that some of its citizens weren't much happier about taxation with representation."

- Lyndon B. Johnson
President, 1963-1969

Milton and Rose Friedman eloquently stated the core tenets of freedom, where *"a society that puts freedom first will, as a happy by-product, end up with greater freedom and equality; [and] though a by-product of freedom, greater equality is not an accident [because] a free society releases the energies and abilities of people to pursue their own objectives, preventing some people from arbitrarily suppressing others"*. He further defined those comments with *"a society that puts equality before freedom will get neither; [but] a society that puts freedom before equality will get a high degree of both"*. In the very same way, the Declaration of our American independence clearly articulated that freedom is fundamentally a self-evident truth – that all people have

187

"certain unalienable rights, that among these are life, liberty, and the pursuit of happiness". As such, government's role is to preserve personal rights, and not to challenge, erode, burden, and diminish

Milton Friedman   **Friedrich Hayek**

individual freedom. Friedrich Hayek's classic 1944 treatise *The Road To Serfdom* warned that a new form of governmental despotism could develop and be implemented entirely in the name of thinking liberally (the true meaning of "liberal" comes from "liberty" – to be "liberated"). His insight was that government could, over time, seek to dictate, legislate, regulate, orchestrate, and even manipulate individuals and private enterprise under the auspices of supposedly ensuring greater *equality* – and in so doing would actually facilitate less equality, while limiting freedom. The key premise of Hayek's perspective is that this road leads backward to serfdom – with less freedoms and greater urdens from a centralized government. We laugh as Michael Palin's iscourse in Monty Python's *Holy Grail* spurned the trappings of udal serfdom with: "King? how'd you get that? by exploiting the orkers and hanging onto outdated imperialist dogma which erpetuates the economic differences in society; you're fooling ourself, we live in a dictatorship, a self-perpetuating autocracy – ipreme executive power is derived by a mandate from the masses, ome and see the violence inherent in the system" – as Terry Jones iys, "we don't have a lord" and responds to Graham Chapman's .sistence the he is their king (Arthur), "well, I didn't vote for you". hat alludes to Hayek's main point, that an entrenched system that rds itself over individual freedom *can* be corrected by a mandate om the masses. The time for such is now.

Hayek understood *"there can be no doubt that most of those in emocracies that demand a central direction of all economic activity still elieve that socialism and individual freedom can be combined"* ternie Sanders believes). Read the inside panel of this book's jacket, President Reagan says: *"All of us want greater fairness, incentives, nd simplicity in taxation; remember, there's no limit to growth and uman progress when people are free to follow their dreams".*

Tax fairness, incentives, and simplicity will remove limits from eedom, growth, and human progress. Without a tax burden, people e more free to pursue individual dreams without having to factor in e waste of compliance, plus having to give over portions of income id gains to the government. Individuals and businesses are then free and unencumbered to plan, invest, create, innovate, manage buy, and sell without limits in potential or execution due to tax an regulatory considerations. The most obvious freedoms we enjoy are:

- Personal choice,
- Uncensored public expression,
- Private property ownership rights,
- Voluntary exchanges, and
- Legal protection under accepted laws.

(There are reasonable limits to unchecked freedom – when publi expression [speech] is a clear and present danger to others, defame another, is publicly obscene, or threatens our nation with violence.)

Sales taxes on every purchase, property taxes on ever structure, federal-state-even city taxes on income, excise taxes o domestic goods, tariffs on imports and exports, mandated payro taxes, capital gains taxes on growth in asset investments, taxes o gifts to others, and taxes due even *after* death all limit our freedom and together have inserted government into virtually every decisio within the American private sector. Having to account for the extr consideration and burden of taxes limits at each juncture ou freedom to dream, think, imagine, create, invest, and decide on th best courses for our personal goals and objectives.

The most obvious negative impacts of taxation that affec individual and business freedom are: 1) altering rational investmen decisions, 2) adding wasted time to enterprising, 3) constraining risk ιking, and 4) diminishing future positive expectations (incentives). ather than simply executing a given investment opportunity, the tax nplications alter freedom of choice by requiring allowances to be ιcluded when addressing the expected tax impacts. The long list of ιquired government regulatory fees, forms, permits, and taxes slow own the pathway to venture development. Risks of creativity and ιnovation must also factor into the burden of tax compliance – both ow and in the future – constraining the risk-taking of individuals to ·y new things. And finally, the future actual results (sales, profit, ιsh flow, gain in value, a patent award) always have to be tempered ownward by the required taxes that will be due on positive future κpectations – disincentives to the freedom of the American dream.

Former House Majority Leader Dick Armey noted "the sheer ιass of our federal government is simply inconsistent with a free ρciety". Even Douglas Amy, founder of *GovernmentIsGood.com* and ιe author of "Capitalism Requires Government" agrees that "some ρvernment activities curtail freedom [as] many laws and regulations ·e inherently coercive, preventing people and organizations from ρing what they want". Jim Powell (Cato Institute) clarified how DR's "New Deal" actually tripled federal taxes in just seven years 933-1940), with the largest revenues coming from excise taxes ιore than the combined individual and corporate income taxes) on ·eryday items like movie tickets, candy, matches, cigarettes, radios, ιaying cards, and alcohol – a huge burden put on the middle-class.

191

An old adage says "the indicator that politicians are lying i this: their mouths are open". The exception is when politicians tal about raising taxes – because then you certainly *can* trust them This book has walked you through the process by which new taxe are conceived, implemented, and typically expanded (more types an at higher rates) over time – but rarely ever cut back or rescinded. Th misguided history of American taxes has introduced multiple layer of additional concerns that truly limit the freedom of individuals t assess, plan for, and ultimately make decisions about personal an business interests, when thinking about saving for a vacation or bi purchase, buying a home or a new car, starting a company, payin for college, investing, or planning for retirement. At every junctur there is a tax due and write-offs to navigate that limit freedoms t pursue what you'd really like to do. The sad commentary is tha most Americans are resolved to the current situation – that taxe limit individual freedom, and nothing can be done about it. The nex chapter presents the case that in addition to limiting freedom, taxe also reduce the upside potential for economic growth

---

Research and analysis sources include: *TaxFoundation.org Mises.org; Library of Economics and Liberty; Richard Anderso "Freedom's Vector: The Path To Prosperity, Opportunity, and Dignity Heritage Foundation; American Spectator; The Freedom Revolutio (Regnery Publishing, 1995); U.S. Constitution; Ronald Reagan nation speech May 28, 1985; AmericanVision.org; Presidency.UCSB.edu*

Chapter 24

Taxes Reduce Economic Growth

Oh, What Those Funds Could Have Produced

*"An income tax form is like a laundry list –
either way, you lose your shirt."*

- Fred Allen
Radio Comedian

If in fact taxes limit personal freedom, is there evidence they also reduce economic growth? Conservatives embrace the position that every dollar spent in the public sector on government programs represents wasted value that could have been more productive in the private sector – building new infrastructure, expanding markets, improving technologies, pursuing R+D, and creating more jobs. The liberal view believes each dollar spent by government helps the economy – by building roads and bridges, doing trade agreements, upgrading IT-systems, underwriting public research grants, and putting people to work in government jobs – all through taxpayer funded programs. There is solid evidence that during periods when taxes were cut (1981, 1986) U.S. GDP had stronger growth and sustained job creation. And in times when taxes and regulations were high, the American economy staggered with little change in GDP and weak employment. The latter defines the recent seven years of President Obama, during which GDP grew at a miserable 2 percent per year (fourth quarter 2015 *real* GDP was up just 7-tenths of one percent according to *Bureau of Economic Analysis* figures released today – January 29, 2016), while over 90 million individuals have exited the labor force, no longer counted in the official *Bureau of Labor Statistics* unemployment rate. Note: the unemployed divided by the total labor force equals *BLS* "U3" unemployment, but does not include those no longer looking for work. When they are added to the unemployed and the total labor force, the "U6" rate captures the true jobs situation. For December 2015, official U3 unemployment was 5 percent, but the true U6 rate was 9.9 percent – twice as high.

The *American Legislative Exchange Council* (ALEC) provides a second set of empirical data at the state level that higher taxes are associated with weak economic growth. Economists Arthur Laffer, Stephen Moore, and Jonathan Williams produce *Rich States, Poor States* (now in its 8th edition) showing consistent trends dating back to 2003 – where states with less of a tax burden tend to have much stronger GDP growth and job creation (lower unemployment). The scoring for each state uses 15 factors such as: top marginal tax rates, property tax and sales tax burdens, GDP, public employees per 1,000 residents, new tax policies and how progressive are tax rates, minimum wage, workers' compensation costs, and unemployment. Prior editions can be viewed at the ALEC website. The best states ıclude: Utah, Wyoming, North Dakota, Arizona, and Texas – the orst states include: New York, New Jersey, Vermont, Minnesota, ınd of course my state of California. While the results are not a erfect correlation, states with the five highest income tax rates California, Hawai'i, Oregon, Minnesota, Iowa) ranked among the ıwest in recent overall performance, as well as the outlook for 2016.

A third way to see how high taxes reduce economic growth is ı examine the Scandinavian countries Denmark, Norway, Sweden, eland, and Finland (often cited as having a high quality of life, low ime, free healthcare, free university education) as shining examples ſ socialism that works. These nations score well on the U.N.'s uman Development Index (HDI) and other "quality-of-life" rankings. residential candidate Bernie Sanders defines himself as a "socialist" ıd regularly refers to "The Swedish Model" that we as Americans ıould learn from. Norway is also often cited as a wonderful example ſ large government with very high taxes and happy "free" people. owever, between 2011 and 2014, high-tax countries Denmark (.25 ercent annual GDP growth), Finland (minus .75), Iceland (2.25), orway (1.6), and Sweden (1.47) have consistently some of the lowest DP rates in the first-world. The Swedish think-tank Timbro ported Finland (5), Sweden (7), and Denmark (10) would rank in ıe bottom-10 in GDP per capita if they were states in the U.S., ıting that high-tax Scandinavian countries have less gross income alaries/wages) and even lower disposable income (after high taxes) an the U.S. Other evidence found these economies function with forms of free market capitalism in their business sectors, whil

Norway benefits from significant oil revenues that together are mor

likely the factors why these nations appear to do well *in spite of* hig

taxes, not *because of* high taxes and massive government programs.

Table 24.1 lists the last 40 years of both U.S. and global GDP.

Table 24.1

COMPARING U.S. GDP TO WORLD GDP
(Trillions of Dollars)

	U.S. GDP	WORLD-GDP	U.S %
1975	$ 1.624	$ 5.801	28%
1980	$ 2.788	$11.052	25%
1985	$ 4.185	$12.445	34%
1990	$ 5.801	$22.921	25%
1995	$ 7.338	$29.693	25%
2000	$ 9.899	$32.240	31%
2005	$12.580	$45.658	28%
2010	$14.587	$63.124	23%
2014	*$17.921*	*$78.281*	*22%*

Source: World Bank Group

It's interesting that American output accounted for almost a third c

the worldwide economy in the mid-1980s (during the PC-revolution

and again in 2000 (the peak of the Internet revolution). Today, th

U.S. is about a fifth of global output, and will be under 20 percent i

just five years. Table 24.2 lists the top ten world economies in 2014

Table 24.2

TOP-10 GLOBAL ECONOMIES
(Trillions of Dollars)

RANK	COUNTRY	GDP
1	United States	$17.92
2	China	$10.38
3	Japan	$ 4.62
4	Germany	$ 3.87
5 ʼ	U.K.	$ 2.95
6	France	$ 2.83
7	Brazil	$ 2.35
8	Italy	$ 2.15
9	India	$ 2.05
10	Russia	$ 1.86

Source: World Bank Group; IMF
World Economic Outlook

.S. GDP slowed in the last 7 years under President Obama to about
percent annually, while taxes went way up. He has proposed a
320 billion tax increase for 2016 that includes raising capital gains
ɪxes to 28 percent. In Ronald Reagan's eight years (during which he
ɪt individual and corporate taxes after the high taxes/slow growth
te-1970s) GDP doubled from $2.7 trillion to $5.4 trillion – an
ɪnual rate of 7.36 percent. During the 8-year tech-boom following
ɪe 1991-92 recession, Bill Clinton had to work with the Republican
ongress to reduce taxes and federal spending, and GDP grew from
ɔ.3 trillion to $9.9 trillion – average annual growth of 5.7 percent.
 can certainly be argued that if, in the aftermath of the 2008
ɪcession, Barack Obama had cut taxes and reduced federal

197

spending, and the economy had expanded at a 5.5 percent average rate (similar to other true recoveries), GDP would have grown from $14.7 trillion in 2008 to $21 trillion by the end of 2015 – instead, i is today only $18 trillion – that's $3 trillion of lost economic growth!

Consider a similar case. Japan's economy was half the size o the U.S. in 1990 ($3.1 trillion vs. $5.9 trillion). Today it's only one quarter the size of the U.S., as very high tax rates, huge governmen spending, and 20 years of near-zero interest (The Bank of Japan jus announced negative interest rates to penalize savings and no spending money) have combined to cripple growth, with GDI averaging only about one percent annually since 2000, including a shrinking economy (negative GDP) in 2008, 2009, 2011, and 2014.

Dozens of studies have found strong relationships between lower taxes and improved GDP. For example, one Canadian stud: (1977-2006) found GDP grew 2-tenths of a percent for each percen reduction in corporate taxes. A U.S. post-WWII study found a on percent cut in individual income tax rates raised per capita GDP 1. percent in the ensuing fiscal quarter, and 1.8 percent after thre quarters. A 1970-2004 study of OECD countries found that highe taxes on individual incomes and corporate profits are the mos damaging factor to an economy, followed in order by deficits an consumption taxes. Another post-WWII study reported a one percen higher tax on GDP leads to a 3 percent drop in output after 2 years very similar to a 2010 IMF study of 15 advanced countries over th prior 30 years. See the TaxFoundation.org for complete details.

Friedrich Hayek wrote that capitalism is the world's only
system of economics compatible with human dignity, prosperity, and
liberty. To the extent we move away from that system, we empower
the worst people in society to manage what they do not understand.
Higher tax rates and more kinds of taxes are a burden to free market
capitalism. Politicians in the past have either cut taxes and reduced
government spending to boost the economy, or have raised taxes and
expanded federal programs only to scratch their heads and wonder
why the economy doesn't do well. Sad to say, many of the latter will
continue to pursue the same tax-and-spend policies believing that
even more government intervention is needed to get the economy
going. The Frenchman Alexis de Tocqueville keenly observed, "I do
not know if the people of the U.S. would vote for superior men if they
ran for office, but there can be no doubt that such men do not run".
It is so important that such a superior candidate be elected in 2016,
to act on the logic that cutting taxes keeps more funds in the hands
of the private sector, to grow the economy and create new jobs. The
final chapter looks at some common sense solutions to do just that.

Research and analysis sources include: *TaxFoundation.org;
Data.WorldBank.org; Democracy In America (de Tocqueville, 1835,
1840); BEA.gov; BLS.gov; ClubForGrowth.org; The Road To Serfdom
(Hayek, 1944); ALEC.org; PewTrusts.org; NBER.org; Heritage.org*

Chapter 25

Common Sense Solutions

Absolutely, This Can Be Fixed

*"It is a paradoxical truth that tax rates
are too high today and tax revenues are too low,
and the soundest way to raise the revenues
in the long run is to cut the tax rates."*

- John F. Kennedy
President 1961-1963

There can be no mistake that the most common sense solutio
to America's misguided history of taxes is not to simply *reform* th
existing system – we have already seen how that has been attempte
several times in the last 40 years, without ever truly fixing the highl
complicated IRS tax code. Instead, we must *replace* the broken IR
tax code with a logical common sense solution. And yet, every tim
someone steps up with a viable proposal to replace the current fiasc
of forms, schedules, rates, and endless regulations, the immediat
reply from politicians is, "It simply can't be done". These argument
love to point out how homeowners will be hurt without the mortgag
interest deduction, and without the charitable donations deduction
will be the end for all non-profit service organizations, and familie

200

must maintain personal and dependent exemptions, without which they won't be able to survive. Next comes the fight to allow medical expense write-offs, followed by deducting state and local taxes paid, and of course, no one could possibly support a new tax plan that doesn't keep in place earned-income credits (EICs) that help lower income families. Add in the major objections from the tax attorneys, tax accountants, and professional tax advisors – and it spells the end of any more discussion on fixing the tax code. The self-fulfilling words win the day – "it simply cannot be done".

The irony in all this remains that whenever new tax provisions or higher rates are proposed for the IRS code, no one ever responds, "It simply can't be done". Instead, expanding regulations, raising tax rates, requiring more paperwork, adding Obamacare penalty taxes, making changes to the existing tax schedules, adjusting credits and exemptions, and increasing the wasted hours and costs of additional compliance are passed along to corporate and individual taxpayers who treat these as normal, within the usual frustrations of American taxes. Why is it then that a plan to *save* time, money, and irritation "cannot be done", but yearly incremental plans that *waste* more time and money with greater exasperation are readily implemented with little or no regard for what's logical, fair, simple, and helpful? When "they" say it can't be done, the American people need to remove all the anonymity from that innocuous pronoun and require "those" naysayers to state very specifically on the record to all U.S. taxpayers WHY they continue to argue that "it cannot be done".

The prevailing great logic behind substantive tax *replacement* i all about being revenue-neutral with the new plan. Perform all of th crazy and convoluted compliance each year, or take 5 minutes to fil a simple one-page form – and if in each case your tax bill was th same, why would anyone care that a previous deduction, exemptior adjustment, or write-off was or wasn't retained? Follow that logi with me. If the current IRS tax reporting, filing, and payment syster requires 20, 30, maybe 40 total hours of time over the course of th year, and costs a person $2,000 - $4,000 - $6,000 or more in lo: time from productive activities at work or home, while also incurrin fees of $1,500 - $2,500 - $3,500 to plan for, strategize, and fil multiple tax forms – and all this results in paying $11,723 in taxes why would anyone not agree to a complete *replacement* of the cod that saves all the time, costs, and fees (and frustration) but ends u with the same $11,723 in taxes? The arguments for the old syster make no sense at all if the *replacement* plan is revenue neutral.

Several studies have pegged tax compliance costs in lost tim (work hours by individuals and businesses), payments for tax advic and preparation, and the costs of forms, software, print, and postag at between $300B and $450B per year. TaxFoundation.org estimate individuals lose 6.6 billion hours per year to tax compliance – th same time as over 3 million people working full-time for 12 month: representing another $200B in wasted productivity. Saving thes costs would then re-inject into the private sector a windfall of a *hal trillion dollars* annually, or $4 trillion of new funds during the ne>

esident's two terms. Our broken tax system brings in $3 trillion ich year, but requires hundreds of deductions, exemptions, and her maneuverings, plus all those wasted hours and fees paid to search and prepare the filings. If that $3 trillion in tax revenue is ie result of around $18 trillion of GDP, that's a 17 percent rate on itional output. Wouldn't it make sense to have a new tax code that illects the exact same $3 trillion (revenue neutral) while saving all ie time, forms, and costs wasted in the current system? That saves er 1 billion tax forms and schedules for the IRS to review, as well those 6.6 BILLION hours spent planning for, and preparing them,

Since 1984, I have consulted to over 500 start-up and emerging ntures. In every case, the entrepreneurs have created or innovated product-service that will save time, be more efficient, save money, ist less, or improve quality. This is called the *value proposition.* hen the time, features, cost savings, and efficiencies are truly :ceptional, we call it a *compelling value proposition* – because it akes no sense to *not* buy this new product or service compared to e current options. That should be the clear objective of any newly oposed tax *replacement* plan – a compelling value proposition that brings in the exact same total revenue with absolutely none of the issle, problems, costs, waste, and frustration. The only people who uld possibly oppose such a *compelling* offer are those entrenched iliticians, special-interest groups, and lobbyists who benefit from e existing hassle, problems, costs, waste, and frustration. But the st majority of American taxpayers would absolutely support it.

So then, what can be done? There are three viable and realistï ways to make this happen. The first is to implement an individuɑ and corporate flat tax with no deductions, exemptions, or speciɑ interest write-offs. Taxpayers simply state pre-tax income, apply th flat rate to find the tax due, and that's it – all on a straightforwaɾ Steve Forbes-style postcard form that takes five minutes to complet(The second option is to completely get rid of all income taxes and pι in place a national value-added tax (VAT) or similar "Fair" tax thɑ works like a U.S. sales tax on daily purchases of goods and servicє that people make all the time. The third option is a combination of flat tax with one of those national consumption-tax formats. In eac case, the IRS would be shut down – phased out over a few transitio years as individuals and corporations settle all prior outstandiɳ taxes and the nation moves over to the new *replacement* plan.

During the 2012 presidential election, two notable proposa made headlines: Herman Cain's "9-9-9" plan, and Gov. Rick Perry "20-20-20". The first stood for a 9 percent flat tax on individuals, th same corporate rate, and a 9 percent national VAT. The second plɑ stood for a 20 percent flat tax on individuals, same for corporation with a balanced budget by 2020. Both would simplify the paperwoɾ and code compliance costs by eliminating extra forms, deduction and credits currently used to reduce gross income to a lower taxab amount on which to calculate taxes due at multiple marginal rates.

The Fair Tax is a revenue neutral plan to replace all individuɑ and corporate income taxes, as well as payroll taxes, with a 2 ercent national consumption tax that will generate the same total of come and payroll taxes currently embedded in prices for goods and rvices (much like excise taxes, the tax burden is spread across the ational population). Founded in 1994, *Americans For Fair Taxation* day reports over 800,000 members nationwide. Most states quote les taxes as *exclusive* – a percentage of the starting price (8 percent 1 $100 price = $108 with the tax). AFFT uses tax *inclusive* terms so e $8 tax is called 7.4 percent of the final $108 price paid. Many gue that the lower 50 percent of taxpayers who pay hardly any (or ro) income taxes, would see their tax burdens increased by paying e fair tax on regular purchases. For example, a 23 percent fair-tax lds $2,300 yearly to individuals or households with purchases taling $10,000. If they currently pay little or no income tax, those 3 percent higher prices are a lot more than what they paid without e new tax. However, corporations paying a lower 23 percent fair tax nd NO income taxes) could easily pass along lower product costs to yers – so those reduced prices are then netted out from the fair tax id. Today's 39 percent corporate tax is already factored into how mpanies price products and services. In 2013, AFFT co-founder ob McNair wrote: *"Instead of a mind-numbing, piecemeal examination ' a tax system that has consistently proven its ineffectiveness, it is ne for Congressional decision makers to cease renovating a broken frastructure, and instead rebuild it; it is time for FairTax"*.

The current presidential candidates all have tax plan proposals. nalysis by the Tax Foundation found that Democrat Bernie Sanders would raise taxes $13.6 trillion in the next 10 years resulting in million fewer jobs. Hillary Clinton's plan raises taxes by a half trillio dollars with 300,000 less jobs. Neither of them is even remote about tax reform, let alone tax replacement – just more of the typic. liberal approach of raising tax rates, expanding who gets taxed, ad more federal deficit spending, and keep increasing the national debt

Many of the Republican candidates (Cruz, Rubio, Bush, Carso propose some form of flat tax, VAT, and/or fair tax, shutting dow the IRS, and cutting the corporate rate down to the 15 percent rang Donald Trump's plan says it applies "common sense" to adju. (reform) the current IRS code by exempting certain income leve from even paying taxes, while eliminating most deductions to ensu that wealthy individuals end up paying at a true 25 percent rate.

The opportunity to make a significant change in the misguide history of American taxes simply requires common sense, the will act, and bold leadership to effect meaningful change that will great reduce the negative impacts the existing IRS tax code has on limitir individual and business freedoms, while also reducing what shou. be strong, sustainable economic growth. People have to tell all the representatives they want change and that "it CAN be done".

This book was intended to walk readers through the history our tax systems at the federal, state, and local levels – showing th. the current structures were not clearly designed in their entirety, b were culled together in highly fragmented pieces over 23 decades ar have no logic in their current forms. Prior attempts at *reform* ha ıly made adjustments to rates, forms, charts, tables, and provisions ıat desperately need *replacement*. If our nation's founders could not ıagine the federal government becoming so invasive as to require its tizens to report and pay taxes on their private incomes and wealth, ıey certainly could never fathom that entire industries of advisors, ıftware, education programs, dispute resolution, and preparation :rvices are devoted to taxes – even college football has a sponsored ıxslayer Bowl with the tagline "Don't Stress This Tax Season".

Replacing the existing tax code will not result in economic crisis ı the markets and industries shift to accommodate a common sense mplified tax code and no IRS. Adjustments happen all the time in ee market capitalism, and this will be no different. Losses to the ofessional tax firms will be overwhelmingly made up for in greater eedoms and increased economic growth from freed-up capital for ıw investments, and the huge savings of formerly wasted time. This ısolutely can be done at this crucial juncture in the life of our great ıtion. So while our tax history has been quite misguided, our tax ture can demonstrate common sense, and help guide America into great new era of expanded liberty and economic prosperity.

:search and analysis sources include: *TaxFoundation.org; ɔnaldJTrump.com; TedCruz.com; MarcoRubio.com; BenCarson.com; ?S.gov; FairTaxNation.com; Forbes.com; Time.com; Washington ɯaminer; AmericansForTaxFairness.org; The Fair Tax Solution (Ken ɔagland, 2010); FoxNews.com; Flat Tax Revolution: Using a Postcard Abolish the IRS (Steve Forbes, 2005); CNN.com; CNBC.com*

E³ FREE MARKET PRESS
SANTA BARBARA ✛ CALIFORNIA

*Follow **David Newton** and **Misguided American Taxes** with the importa⟩ message of this book as it goes nationwide in magazines, book review⟩ web-blogs, talk-radio and television appearances, conferences, chambers commerce, and other speaking engagements up through the 2016 election⟩*

*If you would like to schedule **Dr. Newton** to speak at your event or to your school, civic group, church or temple, political club, college-university class⟩ forum, or business-trade association, contact:* NewtonStrategy@live.com